VOICE YOURSELF
IN THE CLASSROOM

Valerie Bastien
Teacher (OCT) and vocal coach

Find your natural dynamic speaking voice
and maintain it!

Vendera
Publishing

VOICE YOURSELF IN THE CLASSROOM!

ISBN: 978-1-936307-07-4

Cover design: Diana Duhamel
Photography by: Vai Yu Law
Artwork by: Valerie Bastien
Editing Team: Jaime Vendera and Meagan Ruszyk
Interior Layout & Design: Scribe Freelance

This book is dedicated to my grandmother Bernadette for the gift of singing and music. Thank you for your guidance. To my parents who had the brilliant idea of getting me a guitar when I was eight and triggered my love for music: Dad, thank you for teaching me perseverance and creativity. Mom, thank you for showing me kindness and common sense. Thank you both for always supporting me in my career and personal life decisions. To my identical twin sister Julie: Together, we learned the importance of individuality and faith in oneself. Our differences and similarities make us unique and strong. My family, you are the most important people in my life and I am forever grateful to have you by my side every day. To Franc, my best friend forever: Thank you for your unconditional love. Even apart we remain together. To my friend and mentor Jaime Vendera: Thank you for encouraging me to write this book and better myself as an artist.

You inspire me.

Contents

Foreword 7

Teaching 9

PART ONE:
A Complex and Fragile Gift

Chapter One: My Story 12

Chapter Two: The Voice and You 17

Chapter Three: Voice Stereotypes 21

Chapter Four: Vocal Disorders 27

Chapter Five: Voice Yourself! 34

PART TWO:
Understanding the Voice

Chapter Six: The Mechanism Behind the Voice 38

Chapter Seven: Wonderful and Intricate 42

Chapter Eight: Natural and Dynamic 45

Chapter Nine: Raising Your Voice 67

Chapter Ten: Daily Voice Warm-Up 73

PART THREE:
Vocal Health

Chapter Eleven: Maintaining Your Voice 83

Chapter Twelve: Fighting Allergies 98

Chapter Thirteen: Fighting the Common Cold 116

Chapter Fourteen: Voice Loss 139

PART FOUR:
My Classroom

Chapter Fifteen: The Silence Diet 143

Chapter Sixteen: Classroom Management 155

Chapter Seventeen: My Teaching Philosophy 162

Chapter Eighteen: Meditation 173

Wrap-Up! 184

APPENDIX:
Useful Information and Documents

Lesson Plans 187

Glossary 211

Bibliography 216

Acknowledgements 222

Biography 225

By: Jaime Vendera

I fell in love with the voice at a very early age because I discovered that the sound of one's voice had the power to command and own the attention of every person in a room. Since I loved and desired attention, I knew it was a vehicle that I must learn to drive. I discovered this from my stepfather, who had in his possession a soft soothing tone that he varied from low to high, especially when telling me bedtime stories, which created a sense of excitement, wondering what would happen next. He also possessed a robust commanding voice that could control our German Shepard Judah. I loved Judah, but she never listened to my commands like she did my dad's. It wasn't an angry tone that he used that had Judah ready to receive his commands, but rather an authoritative tone that could carry over a football field. I knew one day I would possess such a tone as well.

Growing up, my fascination grew exponentially. In school, I was intrigued by the tones of my teachers. I was amazed by the varieties of colors and dynamics that each individual teacher presented and was puzzled at how a little woman like my English teacher, Mrs. Crabtree, could possess a voice bigger, more lifelike and more commanding than my math teacher, Mr. Maynard. I loved math but Mr. Maynard just couldn't keep my attention, which was probably why my first bad grade in school was in his class. He was authoritative but in a demeaning way, so we all feared him: I don't think we learned what we could from him, nor did we respect him enough to try harder. I am not putting the blame of bad grades upon the teacher, but I do believe it is a contributing factor to helping inspire young minds. For instance, Mrs. Crabtree made me fall in love with writing, which is something I never thought I would ever do at the time.

I truly believe that any student can find the drive to learn and grow through studies if the teacher could only convey passion through their voice—which can be accomplished—with enthusiasm. If only a teacher had the right tools to convey that passion through a variety of tonal color, dynamics and emotional vocal release to keep every single student hanging on their every word while earning their respect.

Many teachers do not understand that the voice is the gateway to reaching every student. Respect is earned through the voice; understanding is earned through the voice, and knowledge is earned through the voice. Still, there is more to it than just varying your pitch. Teachers speak all day long and suffer more than lack of control of their class; suffering from vocal fatigue or worse is not only depressing, but damaging to a teacher's career.

When I was approached by vocal coach/school teacher Valerie Bastien about releasing a book on voice for teachers, I was immediately excited to take on this task and help her finish this project. Voice Yourself in the Classroom is not just a book, I believe it is *the* training manual that *all* teachers should have in their possession—it should be a reading requirement. Although this book is written for teachers of younger children, this book is for anyone who teaches, leads a class, or conducts a workshop. This book will not only show you how to take control of your class, but it will show you how to do it in a healthy manner while protecting your instrument. Be prepared to go back to school and learn how to teach, with total authority and confidence, without losing your voice!

In the teaching profession, vocal issues are a daily reality. When I came to realize how my voice impacted my teaching and my personal life, I started researching the matter to find solutions and cure my voice ailments. Little did I know about how much I would learn and how taking care of my speaking voice would transform me into a healthier and better teacher, and most importantly, how it would make me a happier person.

The idea of writing this book came after I noticed that other colleagues and teachers amongst my family and friends suffered from the same vocal troubles. It was reassuring to know that I wasn't alone but also frightening to realize how helpless most teachers feel about gaining control over their voice. I knew exactly what that felt like, having already been through it. Because I have a singing background, it was fairly easy for me to turn the situation around on my own. However, I thought there was a need for a simplistic approach that anybody can learn from with or without any singing experience whatsoever.

This book was specifically written with teachers in mind. In it, I explain how to coordinate your breath and body in order to produce a healthy natural dynamic speaking voice and maintain it throughout your day. I also share my ideas on classroom management strategies that encourage and sustain an environment where the voice shines. All of the vocal techniques expressed inside the following pages can be applied to both the speaking voice and the singing voice. Of course other voice professionals such as customer service representatives, lecturers, actors, public speakers, politicians, lawyers, radio hosts, amateur and professional singers can also benefit from this book because the speaking voice and the singing voice are the same. The effects that the techniques presented in this book have on your body and your mind are the same. My vocal beliefs can equally be implemented from an educator's point of view, a parent's or anyone else. They are universal. If you are reading this book and you are not a teacher please enjoy this book to its best and take out as much as you can from it but I'm warning you; teachers are the writer's pet this time around!

You only get one set of vocal cords so you've got to use them wisely. The strategies to get there might differ but ultimately the only goal is to maximize the potential beauty of your voice. If you use your voice for a living, as a hobby, or even if you just want to sound nice, this book is for you. Please read on to learn about the voice as an instrument and how you can best care for it. It takes a lot of work, personal willpower, and perseverance to train the voice. Nobody said it would be easy but I know you can do it.

Good luck!

Valerie Bastien

PART ONE
A Complex and Fragile Gift

CHAPTER ONE
My Story

I would like to start off by telling you a bit about myself, and how my experience with the voice evolved over the years. My voice has played an important role in many aspects of my personal life. Some people pretend to have sung their first song around age two or three. I wish I could join the wagon and tell you that I have been singing since I was a baby but that wouldn't be true. My parents weren't singers. I know that my mom can't sing in tune and I have never heard my dad sing at all. However, my maternal grandmother comes from a musical family. She comes from a large family, and in the mid-1900s, music occupied an important place in their lives. Some of her family members played piano and other instruments and they would spend entire afternoons and evenings entertaining themselves by playing music and singing in the living room.

Then my aunt Sylvianne—again on my mom's side—also developed an interest in singing. In the 1960s, she was regularly performing in cabarets around Montreal. She had a wonderfully deep, powerful alto voice that I always admired. I know that I've inherited my vocal qualities from my grandmother's genes and I would say that she and my aunt were my very first influences when it came to singing.

I grew up like any typical child slowly taking interest in singing. I was a quiet child and I was too shy to express myself. I remember my teachers always asking me to speak up to answer questions during class. I loved singing though; and my sister and I enrolled in the village's church choir during holidays. We stood out with our piercing soprano voices, and we were asked to sing solos from time to time. Singing became one of our favorite pastimes. We would often organize mini shows for our family. I even remember composing a song for Mother's Day. Singing was the perfect way for the introverted child that I was to get out of my tiny bubble and confront the world.

When I turned eight, my parents bought my first guitar. I took classical guitar lessons for the next five years. At about the same time, I also started practicing synchronized swimming. I loved playing guitar and I loved swimming, but above all, I loved singing. Learning guitar was really just an excuse to accompany myself. Despite singing remaining my number one passion, interestingly enough, I never thought it necessary for me to take lessons. I thought singing was easy and I could learn on my own. In high school, I continued showing my love for music by participating in several talent shows and decided to pursue my music studies at Vanier College in Montreal, Québec close to the small town where I grew up.

Once again, I underestimated the voice and decided to study classical guitar instead of voice. Luckily, as part of the curriculum, I was required to sing in the college choir. My choir director pushed me into taking voice lessons as my second instrument, which I finally did. Ultimately, I ended up switching to voice as my first instrument and I later graduated with a B.A. in Fine Arts from Concordia University specializing in music performance. I cannot believe I waited so long to realize the voice was a worthy contender of any other instrument. Silly me!

While I was a student, I'd spend my summers in the Old Montreal as a public entertainer on Place Jacques-Cartier. That must have been my best student job. I'd bring my tape player with a pre-recorded tape of piano accompaniments and sang opera arias for passers-by. I made many friends that summer. I was still very timid, but it seemed that as soon as I'd open my mouth to sing, people started paying attention to me. All of a sudden, strangers came up to me wanting to know more about me and it was the most wonderful feeling. At that moment, I understood how powerful the voice could be and I tried to use that to my advantage.

My relationship with the voice continued throughout my professional life. I moved to Toronto in 1995 and found a job doing collections over the phone. My manager soon noticed that my mellow tone was quite effective in handling money requests and especially irate customers. I was promoted to working disputes for the bank's credit card division. Occasionally, customers would tell me out of the blue that I had a beautiful voice. That was always flattering and it put a smile on my face for the rest of the day!

Thus far, all my voice-related experiences were positives. I had no reason to worry about my vocal health until I became a teacher a few years later. My first few years of teaching were pretty rough. I taught French Immersion to students that often didn't seem interested in learning the language and misbehaved. In such conditions, I constantly had to raise my voice to address my class or discipline students. I felt so confident in using my voice that I never stopped to think about whether or not I was doing so properly. I didn't make the connection that if there is a better way to sing, there is also a better way to speak. I didn't know it then but I was clearly misusing my speaking voice and it slowly began to take a toll on me.

I spent the next few years struggling vocally. My throat always felt dry and uncomfortable at the end of the day and I was constantly fighting colds. One year, I caught seven colds in a row between November and March. I lost my voice repeatedly and I missed work several times to rest. When I got home after work, I didn't enjoy singing anymore because my throat hurt so much. I was miserable, and before long, I paid a visit to an ear, nose and throat specialist. My fears were confirmed: he informed me that nodules had started developing on my vocal cords...

I was devastated. How could this happen to me? How could I let this happen? How could I be so naïve and ignore the warning signs? I was a classically trained singer, after all! It didn't take long before I started researching the speaking voice. I read as much as I could on the subject and finally came across a book that put me back on the right path for my speaking voice: *Change Your Voice, Change Your Life* by Dr. Morton Cooper.[1] After reading this book, I understood that my singing voice and speaking voice should be one. This book truly saved my voice and was also a great inspiration for the next several pages you are about to read.

I have since come to a few conclusions about the voice:

1. To sing, you must want to sing and you must love to sing. The love of singing is important whether you are singing at the age of two or eighty-two.

2. EVERYONE should seek some sort of background concerning the voice. We ALL use our voice everyday and I am living proof that the speaking voice can be more harmful than the singing voice. Never did I lose my voice once during singing, but once I became a teacher, my speaking voice almost cost me my singing voice. And...

3. Your voice is you. You need to discover who YOU are.

The speaking voice and the singing voice are whole and an integral part of one's personality and lifestyle. To achieve balance while juggling self-esteem, authority, creativity, stress,

---

[1] Cooper, Dr Morton. <u>Change Your Voice, Change Your Life</u>. New York, NY. Macmillan, 1984

expectations, heartaches, joy, and beauty, you use the voice as a compelling asset. Aligning the voice with the needs of your emotions, daily activities and career has to come from a natural and comfortable place. Only then, can you truly glow, perform your best and inspire. We are role models for one another and especially greatly influential on students. I urge you to discover and define the nature of your being through finding your natural dynamic voice. Learn to embrace the challenges that all the segments of your life (and specifically education for the purpose of this book), have to offer. The first step in the right direction starts here! Congrats, you already are on your way....

CHAPTER TWO
The Voice and You

At this point, you're probably thinking to yourself, "This sounds really nice but I'm no singer." Well, even if you can't sing to save your life, fear not. That won't be a problem in finding your natural dynamic speaking voice. It doesn't matter at all whether your singing voice sounds horrific or wonderful. I wrote this book with teachers in mind, although many of the concepts discussed are relevant to anyone that uses his or her voice professionally.

The Merriam-Webster online dictionary defines *to sing* as follows: "to produce musical tones by means of the voice, to create in or through words a feeling and to give information or evidence."[2] In comparison, it also describes *to speak* as follows: "to utter words or articulate sounds with the ordinary voice and to express thoughts, opinions, or feelings orally."[3] Just like songs, your speech pattern is made out of spoken words on different inflections.

If you don't have the skills to produce enough modulations in your range to actually sing a song and consider yourself a singer, nothing stops you from incorporating some singing elements on a smaller scale into your speaking voice. To me, this is what speaking is all about: singing on a much smaller scale. Both speaking and singing are about manipulating and varying the pitch, dynamic and tone of the voice. Again, you don't have to be a singer to use your vocal cords properly. It's

---

[2] "Sing", <u>Merriam-Webster Online</u>. October 10th, 2010. <http://www.merriam-webster.com/dictionary/sing>
[3] "Speak", <u>Merriam-Webster Online</u>. October 10th, 2010. <http://www.merriam-webster.com/dictionary/speak>

like how you pluck the strings of a guitar without them breaking and without ever knowing how to play a complete tune.

It doesn't matter if you have a limited range. It doesn't matter if you can't sing in tune because this book is about finding your speaking voice for the classroom through realizing that your voice IS an instrument. You should still perceive your voice as the ideal instrument and your words as a musical means to get people's attention because everything is music. Music is everywhere and music is the most powerful tool you will ever have to express yourself. It only takes a few seconds to realize the omnipresence of music on earth and its outmost importance.

For example, take the birds whistling or the soothing melody of the ocean waves on the beach. Even the thunder roar is melodious if you care to listen. Music is also heard in the streets when cars honk at each other. The television set in your home provides a subtle music background to the disjointed playing noises of too many forks, knives and spoons held in your hands while setting up the table. As you walk down the street on your way to school in the morning and supervising the yard during recess, can you hear the joyful screams of children playing until the bell interrupts their wonderful symphony?

Finding the beauty on all sounds depends on how you look at them in your surrounding. Some music composers make it a point to use non-traditional instruments found in our environment to perform musical pieces. I had the privilege of going to one of these events in 1995, as I was still studying at University of Montreal. It was part of my class to report on Canadian contemporary music performances. One of the concerts I attended took place in the Old Port of Montreal. It was a Harbour Symphony, written by Paul Steffler and Don Wherry. I wish I could take you back in time to experience the creative energy of hundreds of ship horns honking rhythmically and sometimes disorderly, one after the other followed by the occasional sound of a train whistle and special occurrences of the bells of Basilica of Notre-Dame.

It was magical to hear this huge fanfare meticulously orchestrated to echo endlessly all over the city. I'm grateful to have been part of the audience that day because this unique music piece opened my eyes on the diversity and infinite possibilities of music. It was truly spectacular.

Can you see how everything is music and how music is everywhere? Music can be found in the least expected places. What better place than within yourself to start your search for music and harmony? Tune yourself to music to find harmony in your life. You might not have considered yourself a singer before but in some way, everybody is to a certain degree. Vibration is the source of life. Since every object and being is made of atoms and atoms create vibrations that explains why the voice has such a powerful influence on you and the people around you. The vibrations you create and live in have such a profound effect on your behavior and the lives you touch. Unless you were born without vocal cords, you must acknowledge and accept your singing and speaking voice as a force to be reckoned with!

Just like the creative effort expressed in the orchestra on water music composition, finding your most beautiful and natural dynamic speaking voice is not an eccentricity; it's a gift that you owe to yourself. What I mean is find the simplest music in you, perhaps the most unlikely place you would have expected it to be, and bring out the best there is! If you have a restricted singing range, you can still make your speaking voice sound great without any pain. You have the full potential of using your vocal cords the same way a professional singer would and apply similar strategies to your speech pattern. In fact, you probably naturally did at one point in your life without even knowing it. Yes, you did... when you were a baby! Before you even knew how to coordinate your tongue, lips and jaw to articulate words, what did you do? You cried and you screamed, just like every baby cries and screams so loud without ever hurting their vocal cords. Have you ever heard of a baby that had lost his voice from screaming so loudly? The odds of that happening are very slim! This tells us a lot. We all start our life using our vocal cords correctly and then we change. Why? Ponder the answer as we move onto the next chapter...

CHAPTER THREE
Voice Stereotypes

We all start our life using our vocal cords correctly and then we change because of our natural nature to model good and bad examples around us. Parents help us learn non-verbal communication first; then they teach us to feed ourselves, walk, use the toilet and talk. Quickly enough, we learn to write, read and count at school, et cetera. Has it ever occurred to anyone that using the speaking voice properly should be taught at an early age, too? I'm a primary school teacher, and already at age five and six, I hear students misusing their voice. I can only fear for what they will sound like as adults. But we learn through imitation, and therefore, we are most likely to repeat the voice patterns around us, good or bad. If nobody ever takes the time to address this issue, the notion of what the correct speaking voice sounds like remains ignored and a positive example is therefore pretty close to impossible to purposely replicate.

Nature has given a certain kind of voice; that voice represents the spirit, the soul, the heart, the intellect... everything that is in man.[4] However, there is no denying of the great pressure in our society to look and behave a certain way. We all are victims of falling under their weight and we grow up more or less aware of expectations put upon us by our family, friends, people we report to, and the media. As far as the speaking voice is concerned, there is definitely a correlation between the kind of personality one is trying to convey and the sound of one's voice. It is natural to model your voice after someone you admire

---

[4] Khan, Hazrat Inayat. The Mysticism of Sound and Music. Delhi, India. Motilal Banarsidass Publishers Private Limited, 1990, p. 87

whether consciously or not, for specific purposes. However, this is where the dangers lie and voice stereotypes leading to vocal misuse come into play. Let's examine different voice types so that you have a full understanding of the music that can be played with your instrument.

THE LOW VOICE

Many people seem attracted towards speaking with a low voice and so it appears extremely popular. For some reason, people falsely attribute different qualities to it. For example, the low voice seems to make news anchors sound serious and believable. I'm sure you've heard a person with a low voice that made you immediately think "Wow, that person has a radio voice..." The low voice makes an ordinary man sound virile and charming. It makes a politician sound credible and knowledgeable. It makes a teacher sound assertive and authoritative, which I can personally relate to. I actually learned to use a low voice to assume my assertiveness long before becoming a teacher. I think the next story is worth telling even though it might come across as unrelated, but if you keep reading, you will understand the point I'm trying to make.

More than ten years ago, my husband and I bought a little puppy; a Yorkshire Terrier that we named Neptune. He was so tiny and cute! Really, he was adorable... at first! We soon found out that terriers have a reputation for being a dominant breed and Neptune was no exception. Very early on, he started snapping at us when we'd try to comb his beautiful, silky long hair or growl when we'd try taking his toys away from him. We didn't quite know what to do about it.

One day, my husband was taking a walk with his mom in Westmount (Montreal, Qc). He happened to walk by a man with an incredibly obedient German Shepherd. My husband was so impressed that he turned around and engaged in a conversation with him. The stranger turned out to be a McGill pet psychology student. We made an appointment with him and he came to our house to teach us how to train our puppy.

Upon arrival, without saying a word, he tested Neptune's behavior by grabbing his muzzle, holding him on his side on the ground and by holding him on his back in his arms like a baby. I remember Neptune to be extremely furious and upset by it all. He was growling at him like crazy! I also remember the student pet psychologist saying that he had not trained small breeds before and that he was surprised to see how mean an eight-pound dog could appear. He prescribed a strict daily routine of exercises, which consisted of grabbing the dog's muzzle, putting the dog on his side on the ground or holding him in our arms for a few seconds like he had demonstrated. We were instructed to do this with our dog at least twice a day. The student pet psychologist had more advice: during the exercise, we absolutely had to teach Neptune what behavior was or was not acceptable to us so he could submit to our commands.

This is where my story becomes relevant to the subject at hand: The type of voice was crucial when communicating our feelings to our dog. He instructed us to use a soft, high pitch voice to express approval, pride and to reward the dog. A loud, low pitch voice was preferred to discipline the dog and show our anger if he were to growl or snap at us. The student pet psychologist even mentioned that dogs usually submit to men more easily since they have lower voices compared to women and children in general. All of that made a lot of sense. We applied his recommendations and were very successful in training our little angel.

Using my voice that way became second nature and I unconsciously applied the same principles when teaching. If I were unhappy about something happening in my classroom, I'd use a low voice. With time, I started using a low voice more and more regardless of my state of mind but rather as part of my attempt to establish myself as trustworthy, respectable and in command in the classroom. The problem with that is speaking with a low voice is, for most of us, unnatural and unsafe for the vocal cords. It focuses the resonance of the voice in the throat.

Speaking of the vocal cords, maintaining a low voice all the time can actually irritate the vocal cords because you aren't giving them the flexibility that changing your voice from low to high allows. Speaking in one area such as the low voice for long periods of time may result in vocal damage such as nodules. I'm pretty sure that is the reason why I started developing nodes during teaching.

THE HOARSE VOICE

There is a difference between a hoarse voice resulting from a cold and people purposely creating that effect on their voice when speaking. The first one is unintentional but both can lead to serious vocal damage. Think of a cool radio host ready to rock. Think of the narrator of your favorite movie trailer trying to sound at times scary, at times exciting. This type of voice has become amazingly trendy, seeming to give whoever uses it an edge. It portrays defiance and assertiveness both packaged in some kind of rock star attitude. The hoarse voice has a lot of grit and definitely sounds scratchy and sometimes smoky because it does exactly that—it scratches your vocal cords and uses too much air.

Beware that the hoarse voice and the low voice often go hand in hand. Sometimes, you'll hear people using so much rasp and bass in their voice that it almost sounds ridiculous! Many grit advocates in the music world know of non-destructive techniques that will protect your vocal cords from damage. Even if some people are successful at using grit safely, I personally don't want to take that chance. Use at your own risk!

THE BREATHY VOICE

The breathy voice is simply characterized by someone letting too much air flow through the vocal cords. Some women even speak in a whispery and childlike voice to portray the breathy sound. It is known to make a woman sound sexy and attractive. I'm not sure why that is, maybe because it was Marilyn Monroe's signature sound? Or perhaps it gives a false impression of youthfulness and naïveté? One thing is sure; a breathy voice is unhealthy for your vocal cords. Too much air will quickly dry them out and make your throat feel uncomfortable. Less hydration means less elasticity and that too prevents the vocal cords from vibrating freely. It can lead to future vocal complications as well.

THE NASAL VOICE

The nasal voice is easily recognizable and reinforced by many regional accents. While some can't tolerate it, others embrace it. In traditional folklore and storytelling, it is often associated with villains such as witches or Dr. Evil in the Austin Powers movies, for example. It is the only type of voice that does not incur damage to the vocal cords. It might be perceived as unpleasant, even annoying, but because it places the voice's resonance high in the nose, there is no unnecessary pressure on the vocal cords while they vibrate. The nasal voice occurs when you push that palate sensation forwards and pinch it up in the nose. At times it can feel like you are squeezing in the roof of your mouth like trying to say "urrrr". This is how the singer Scott Stapp from Creed gets his sound. What we are looking for instead is to move the nasal focus upward to beautify and fully unveil the potential of one's voice. To know if your voice sounds nasal when you speak, pinch your nostrils. If the tone changes, your voice is too nasal.

THE HIGH VOICE

There are some people who talk too high; that can cause damage, too. The larynx will want to go up and down during speech inflection if the voice is too high and not at its natural pitch because it's not trained for that range. It takes quite good control to stabilize the larynx properly in order to achieve enough room for the vocal cords to, again—and I apologize for sounding redundant here—vibrate freely.   Aesthetically speaking, too much of a high voice sounds out of character for a grown-up. It obviously sounds effeminate for a man but mostly it sounds phony. To me, when someone uses an exaggerated high pitch voice, I think he or she is trying to fool me for some reason. For example, I hate it when I go to a family restaurant and the waiter or waitress speaks to me with an unnatural high pitch voice. Instead of convincing me that the food I will order is good, I think he or she knows better and being overly friendly is to compensate on service!

Any of these negative voice patterns can become so ingrained in us that they become part of ourselves. We get so accustomed to hearing ourselves speak a certain way that the actual correct voice comes across as the impersonator.   Don't be fooled! Which one of these voices are you? If you recognized yourself in these types of voices, chances are you might sooner or later have to live with some health consequences unless YOU change! Now that you understand how detrimental your approach to the speaking voice can be on your vocal health, let's discuss what can occur from vocal misuse in the next chapter.

CHAPTER FOUR
Voice Disorders

Misusing the voice can have significant repercussions on your physical and mental health. Speaking seems so natural that we sometimes forget how fragile the vocal cords actually are. According to research performed by The Denver Center for the Performing Arts and National Center for Voice and Speech, teachers' vocal cords vibrate a cumulative average of 23% of their time at work; that is about one hour and 50 minutes of voicing for eight hours of work.[5]

Depending on your teaching style and the subject you teach, you could expect to see your personal average increase dramatically. I personally estimate that I spend much more time speaking than that due to the nature of teaching second languages to young children; and you most possibly are, too. The truth is, vocal cords probably are your best friends in the classroom. Let's face it: they are the number one tools in expressing your ideas. Still, we tend to underestimate their importance and overestimate their strength. It doesn't come as a surprise that most teachers experience vocal disorders at some point during their career.

Besides misusing and overusing the voice, there are two other ways people incur voice problems: catching colds or the flu and smoking. I will share with you my tips on fighting the common cold and flu virus in chapter thirteen. While there is sometimes close to little we can do to avoid getting sick, the second one, smoking more or less is on the other hand a deliberate way to

---

[5] Hunter, Eric J. "153rd ASA Meeting, Salt Lake City, UT. -How Much Do Teachers Talk? Do They Ever Get a Break?" Acoustical Society of America. October 10th, 2010. <http://www.acoustics.org/press/153rd/hunter.html>

harm the voice. I know that addiction to smoking is very difficult to reverse but you have to know that cigarettes are probably the voice's greatest enemy. You are most likely already aware of the dangers associated with smoking and its related cancer risks.

It is tobacco smoke rather than nicotine that is the most harmful to the voice and the main cause of cancer of the mouth, throat, lungs, and esophagus. Smoke from marijuana is as toxic if not worst.   Don't do drugs!   Heat also bears some responsibility in their danger to the breathing and voice apparatus. The throat is covered by a thin lining of hair like cells called cilia where dirt particles from the polluted air is trapped and carried through the breathing and digestive tract. One puff prevents the larynx from naturally re-hydrating itself for at least 3 hours. Consequently, hydration being detrimental to a healthy larynx, irritation starts. Redness, swelling and dryness of the throat should be expected if you smoke. An increase of mucus secretions would also be simultaneously noticed along with a lack of hydration in addition to the thickening of the surface lining of the larynx. Over time, white stains can appear in the throat; a clear sign of cancer slowly developing. Yellow teeth, bad breath and smelly fingers can be socially unattractive. Over time, a smoker's voice becomes hoarse and looses tone clarity. A shrinking range and shortness of breath are also most likely to occur. Finally, years of smoking turns lungs completely black. A truly scary sight!

Also think about your role in setting a positive example for kids. Teachers have a special place in the heart and eyes of the community. The image we convey with our words and actions on a health and moral level is considerable and should not be taken lightly. Being a teacher is a 24/7 affair. It is a non-stop process. There is no break from how people of your community perceive you so make sure to use that power wisely. Many of the disorders described below can result from smoking. So again smoking is obviously strongly discouraged for many understandable reasons!

There are several conditions associated with the voice but I will only describe the ones that seem the most pertinent to teachers and their speaking voice.

DISCLAIMER: I do not intend in any way to diagnose any condition that you may or may not have based on the definitions below. If you have any concerns, please consult your family doctor or an ear, nose and throat specialist.

Laryngitis: *inflammation of the vocal cords inflicted by a virus, bacteria or misuse of the voice.* Laryngitis is the most common condition and is often a complication of what seemed to have started as a simple cold. Repeated contact with smoke, acid reflux and chemicals can also be held responsible for laryngitis. It is very important to show special care for the voice under attack because the swollen vocal cords constantly irritating one another might lead to unwanted tension and consequently develop long-term disorders such as vocal nodules, polyp or cysts.

Vocal Nodules: *small growth resembling tiny hard bumps forming on both vocal cords.* During vocal misuse, the cords rub each other, creating tension while they vibrate. Similarly to a callous, they will form exactly at the spot on the vocal cords where the most pressure has been applied.

Polyp: *tissue growth on one or both of the vocal cords that could be compared to a blister because of its soft* *texture filled with fluid.* Tobacco use is most often associated with the occurrence of a polyp although, once again, voice overuse alone can generate it. Polyps can appear even after a single traumatic incident such as coughing violently or screaming on the top of your lungs during a rock concert.

Contact Ulcer: *a sore developing on a vocal cord.* This kind of injury can occur in someone that often shouts and raises their voice or if suffering from gastro-esophageal reflux.

Bowed Cords: *there is a gap between the two vocal cords as they fail to come together completely and the air flows through.* One or both the cords might appear bowed. It is typically characterized by a breathy voice.

Spasmodic Dysphonia: *involuntary muscle spasms make it difficult for the vocal cords to adduct and therefore sound is not produced adequately.* The vocal cords become stiff and don't open to vibrate properly. Its cause is unknown. Although this condition can be inherited, it is certainly worsened by stress.

Vocal Cord Paralysis: *one or both the vocal cords are paralyzed.* A viral infection or other traumas such as neck injuries, cancer and strokes can cause the paralysis. This can be a life threatening condition because when the cords refuse to close, liquid and food can fall through the airways and provoke chocking.

Many voice related conditions can be treated with proper voice therapy. In extreme cases, surgery might be necessary to rectify the situation. Only a doctor can diagnose whether this would be called for. You probably intuitively already know whether you display minor or serious symptoms of voice disorders worth requiring professional advice from a doctor. If you want a more holistic venue to rehabilitate your voice, I can help! On the next page, I have created a short questionnaire to help you discover the current state of your own voice and figure out if you're at risk of developing symptoms of vocal abuse.

SELF-EVALUATION

Answer the following questions by "yes" or "no" to find out.

1. Would you say that you spend most of your day talking? ☐ Yes ☐ No

2. Do you have difficulty being heard in a noisy environment or above a crowd, forcing you to raise your voice or shout to address your class? ☐ Yes ☐ No

3. Do you use a low-pitched voice to discipline students or when you're upset? ☐ Yes ☐ No

4. Do you sometimes whisper in an attempt to "save" your voice? ☐ Yes ☐ No

5. Do you often feel like you need to clear your throat? ☐ Yes ☐ No

6. Does your throat feel dry after a lesson? ☐ Yes ☐ No

7. Do you feel any pain in your neck area at the end of your school day? ☐ Yes ☐ No

8. Do you ever wake up with a sore voice without being "sick" per se? ☐ Yes ☐ No

9. Do you sometimes feel that your voice is better in the morning and becomes weaker in the afternoon? ☐ Yes ☐ No

10. Do you often catch a cold or the flu? ☐ Yes ☐ No

11. Are you an avid coffee drinker? ☐ Yes ☐ No

12. Do you have a breathy voice? ☐ Yes ☐ No

13. Would you describe your voice as hoarse? ☐ Yes ☐ No

14. Do you smoke? ☐ Yes ☐ No

15. Do you feel self-conscious about your voice? ☐ Yes ☐ No

If you answered "yes" to ANY of these questions, you're at risk of developing vocal problems in the near future unless you attend to this issue as soon as possible. The good news is that with proper voice training, chances are your vocal problems can be remedied faster than you think! And please, please, please: If you worry that you may be experiencing any of the symptoms described in this section, visit your family doctor or an ear, nose and throat specialist as soon as possible. It would be my pleasure to accompany you through the process of finding your natural dynamic voice and maintain it so that you can "Voice Yourself in the Classroom" and be heard! Let me explain why that is so important.

CHAPTER FIVE
Voice Yourself!

Yes, vocal cords are an incredible asset in the classroom. They are the finest vehicle to convey your ideas. Whether it's to share your knowledge or for classroom management, students are more likely to listen to you if you have a clear, confident and beautiful voice. Your voice never lies. It truthfully carries out your emotions and your personality. It's the best lie detector there is!

Better control over your voice will allow you to remain authentic while remaining in command of your emotions. You cannot be taken seriously when you copy someone else's voice consciously or not. Don't be someone you're not. Don't fall into the traps of the most common clichés. A rock star (low or hoarse voice), a sexy lady (breathy voice), Dr. Evils (nasal voice), a fake (high voice); is that really who you want to be... in the classroom?

After all, you are who you are. You don't need to sound cool. You don't need to sound sexy. You don't need to shout, scream, and sound loud in order to get the respect and attention of your class. Actually, you generally don't need to be loud to be respected and listened to. However, there is a way to strengthen your voice and project it naturally without becoming unnecessarily loud, which could damage the voice. Increasing your volume is an integral part of this program. So not to worry, although loud is not always recommended, I will still teach you how to increase your volume later!

All of that is to say, don't give in to the pressure of sounding a certain way to meet expectations that wouldn't do you and your vocal cords any good. The only way you need to sound is: positive! Use your voice positively to create a kind, smart, and fun image of yourself: One that people will be attracted to and want to be associated with, and a voice that your students will recognize as compassionate and understanding. Use your voice to create opportunities and make the best out of your teaching abilities. Here is what my young friend Tristan Cook, a private music teacher from Ontario (Canada), had to say about the voice:

> "Tone truly makes a universe of difference. With a happy, open and encouraging tone, a student will latch on and their performance will match it. They will play the best they can. If you aren't being positive, I wish you luck in creating a positive experience."

This applies to any areas of teaching. In my opinion, the voice is the most wonderful, powerful and intricate instrument of all. It is God-given. It is a gift. Nobody sounds like you and you don't sound like anybody else. It deserves your full attention so your uniqueness can shine throughout. I will help you find out how to gain control over your voice. I love this quote from Oscar Wilde that pretty much sums up my state of mind: "Be yourself, everybody else is taken!" Before we move on to how the voice works and now that you know the dangers of misusing your voice, here's a basic picture of what your voice SHOULD be:

Confident

Inviting

Positive

Nurturing

Assertive

Calm

Natural

Authentic

Beautiful

Free

PART TWO
Understanding the Voice

CHAPTER SIX
The Mechanism Behind the Voice

Understanding the mechanism behind the voice is fundamental to successfully produce your natural dynamic speaking voice. I will try to simplify how the voice works for you. There are three essential components to your instrument. On its website, The Watergate Voice Foundation[6] describes them as the air pressure system, the vibratory system, and the resonating and modifying system. Let's discuss all three:

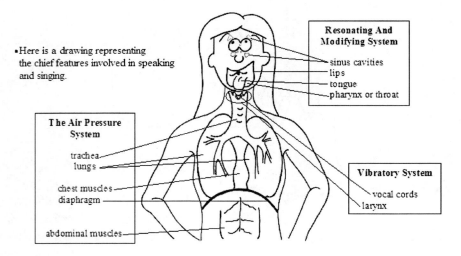

• Here is a drawing representing the chief features involved in speaking and singing.

Resonating And Modifying System
- sinus cavities
- lips
- tongue
- pharynx or throat

The Air Pressure System
- trachea
- lungs
- chest muscles
- diaphragm
- abdominal muscles

Vibratory System
- vocal cords
- larynx

THE AIR PRESSURE SYSTEM
When you inhale, your diaphragm—assisted by the muscles around your rib cage and in your abdomen—controls how much air is drawn in before it's released out of your lungs and through your trachea. The diaphragm expands in a dome-like shape

[6] "Anatomy and Physiology of Voice Production", <u>The Voice Problem Website</u>. October 10th, 2010. <http://www.voiceproblem.org/anatomy/index.asp>

during inhalation and relaxes or shrinks back up during exhalation.

The force at which the air is sent back up your trachea and through closed vocal cords determines the amplitude at which they vibrate to create various dynamics. The diaphragm, is a flat muscle that is attached to the bottom front, sides and back of the lungs. It controls the pressure needed during breathing, speech or singing. To speak loudly, considerable pressure is required while the opposite is true to speak softly.

THE VIBRATORY SYSTEM

Next, the airflow continues its way up through the larynx, which is where your vocal cords are. A thin layer of mucus covers these tiny frail muscles. Their back and front extremities are attached to the larynx. Also referred to as the voice box, the larynx includes a wide variety of cartilages and muscles, which I'm not going to bore you with. The vocal cords lay horizontally in a "V" shape, below your Adam's apple (though more noticeable in men, women also have one) with the narrow part at the front of your larynx. They are not engaged during normal breathing and therefore remain wide open. To generate an actual sound, the vocal cords gently close together and start vibrating as the air is expelled from the lungs. During sound inflection, your voice box slightly tilts forward and its back expands upward and probably sideways too, delicately pulling the vocal cords. The higher the sound, greater is the angle and the tension. That increases or decreases the length of the vocal cords, and in turn, generates higher or lower pitches.

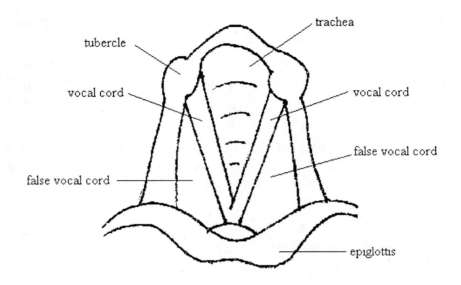

The narrow part of the "V" formed by the vocal cords is attached by the Adam's apple. This side is therefore the front of the neck!

THE RESONATING AND MODIFYING SYSTEM

Your voice is manipulated into words with the help of your tongue and lips. You can direct the sound of your voice in different parts of your head and throat. First, it can resonate in your throat, which is sometimes called the pharyngeal voice. If not careful, the voice can resonate down low in the throat, which is evident by a vocal fry like tone. This is wrong and we want to stay away from this sound. If you've ever heard anyone say: "His voice is down in his throat!", it wasn't a compliment. It can also resonate a little higher in your mouth or much higher in your nasal cavities. The latter is of most interest to us. The nasal cavities consist of your sinuses between and above your eyes and around your cheeks. This area of your face is called "the mask". This is where you want to focus your resonance to favor enough elongating of your vocal cords so they can vibrate

freely without rubbing and hurting each other. How to focus
that tone there? I will tell you how to do this shortly.

Here is another one of my artistic renditions! See in detail
the vibratory, resonating and modifying systems.

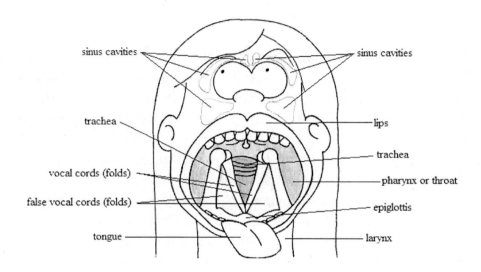

What is resonance? Resonance simply is the cumulative
energy derived from frequencies produced by your vocal cords.
It is your voice vibrating against the walls of your instrument,
your body. Your body becomes a tuning fork for powerful waves
of sounds echoing and reverberating endlessly when you talk
and sing.

To sum up, the breath activates the voice. During
exhalation, the diaphragm controls how much air pressure is
required to produce a sound. Then, vocal cords vibrate, gently
elongating back and forth according to the inflection of the voice
intended. Its resonance momentarily finds refuge against the
cavities of your chest, neck and head before your tongue and jaw
carefully form the sounds into words as they come out of your
mouth for the world to hear, enjoy and appreciate! The voice is
at once wonderful and intricate and I will tell you why...

CHAPTER SEVEN
Wonderful and Intricate

Did I tell you how much I love the voice? I'm completely fascinated by it. It is the only God-given music instrument. The human voice is one of the smallest instruments on Earth but it amazes by its versatility and power. It vibrates to create (in conjunction with the rest of the vocal box) an array of sounds like no other conventional musical instrument can. It's a jewel sitting in the back of your throat!

Your vocal cords are special in the way that nobody else has the same length and thickness as yours. Or if somebody did, the odds of also having the same variables of body size, trachea size, shape of surrounding muscles and cavities are close to impossible. That is why we all sound different. I am a living proof of that. I have an identical twin sister and we don't quite sound the same; similar but still different. All these attributes are in part responsible for your own unique tone and color. They help to shape your personality. The voice also comes with its own amplification system activated by the breath. Breathing is life. Life is about connecting with your inner self and people around you and hence, our favorite means of communication.

Healing powers are even attributed to the resonating voice in some Eastern cultures. Why is the voice so powerful? Because it comes from music and music is the divine source of life and non-living things on Earth. The power of vibration is surprisingly unknown and underestimated. Every being and object on earth is made of molecules and therefore vibrates. Every thought, every move, every sound is vibration. As far as I'm concerned, there is no such thing as silence. Music is all around you, from the heartbeat of an unborn child and the quiet hush of your nervous system to the rain falling down and the clock's *tick-tock* hanging on your classroom wall. When you speak, your vocal cords vibrate on average between 110 and 300 times per second.[7] The energy generated travels in your entire body and can touch the lives of many before and after it comes out of your mouth. The great Sufi leader, Hazrat Inayat Khan, says that, "a friendly person shows harmony in his voice, his words, his movements and manner. An unfriendly person, in all his movements, in his glance and expression, in his walk, in everything, will show disharmony."[8] He also considered the science of sound to be the most important science to use in every condition of life: in healing, in teaching, in evolving, and in accomplishing all things in life.[9] My very good friend and mentor, Jaime Vendera[10] (a world-renowned vocal coach, author and the only documented person to ever shatter glass with his voice without amplification), once told me that we must speak every word from a point of internal emotional happiness in order to allow the voice to vibrate at its best resonance. In the same train of thought, people sing when they're happy or when they want to channel their sadness or anger in order to find solace. That is wonderful to me. Thus, your voice (inner voice or spoken) is your greatest strength. Choose your thoughts, your words and your voice carefully and you will discover the tremendous potential and the power it gives you and the people around you. This is the best-kept secret of all time!

---

[7] "Anatomy and Physiology Of Voice Production: Understanding How Voice Is Produced", The Voice Problem Website. October 10th, 2010.
<http://www.voiceproblem.org/anatomy/understanding.asp>
[8] Khan, Hazrat Inayat. The Mysticism of Sound and Music. Delhi, India. Motilal Banarsidass Publishers Private Limited, 1990, p. 13
[9] Khan, Hazrat Inayat. The Mysticism of Sound and Music. Delhi, India. Motilal Banarsidass Publishers Private Limited, 1990, p. 77
[10] Vendera, Jaime. "Jaime Vendera : World Class, Glass Shattering Vocal Coach". Jaime Vendera. October 10th, 2010. <www.jaimevendera.com>

Tune yourself to your voice to create a strong learning environment for your classroom. I want you to fully benefit from your own vocal magic. The voice is unique in the way that, unlike any other music instruments, you cannot see or touch it. It is intended to be used in a certain way, but without your instrument in front of you, it is pretty challenging to play it properly. The vocal cords are meant to vibrate freely and produce the most beautiful sound you have ever heard. Remember: if your instrument breaks, you cannot buy a new one at the nearest local music store. I cannot reiterate enough how important it is that you treat your voice as one of the most valuable components of your physical and psychological health.

No wonder this fragile treasure hidden in the back of your throat requires special care and attention! All of what you have read so far was a preamble to the coming chapter. In the next pages, you will learn different methods to help you find your natural dynamic speaking or singing voice. Read on!

CHAPTER EIGHT
Natural and Dynamic

I have described a few common voice stereotypes that lead to negative repercussions, I have explained the mechanism behind the voice, and I have tried to pass on to you my passion for the voice. Now, I want to tell you how to use your voice correctly. It's simple: you must find your natural dynamic speaking voice. My principal, Liliana Sarno from Ontario (Canada), explains how she once received vocal advice when she was studying to become a teacher but didn't really see the value in it until later in her career:

"When I was at University of Toronto in the Faculty of Education, we had two sessions with a voice coach. She gave us some exercises to do, which were designed to strengthen our voices and to help us project our voices. We all thought it was quite silly at the time. Of course now I wish that I had practiced them more. Being a Core French teacher and later a Phys. Ed. and Family Studies teacher, I would regularly lose my voice in Term One, especially in September."

I am sure that my principal took some of these advices in at some point or another in her career because she has a beautiful speaking voice today and she tells me all the time how she loves to sing! So please don't underestimate your voice! Read through the following chapters and start applying my suggestions daily. There are three steps to follow in order to find your natural, dynamic speaking voice. First, breathe properly to support the voice. Second, keep your larynx and tongue relaxed during elocution. Third, place the voice into its natural resonators.

BREATHING AND SUPPORTING THE BREATH

Breath is gas for your engine. If your breathing is off, everything else will be too. You must concentrate to breathe deeply and keep your body relaxed. Usually, singers breathe either by the nose or mouth alternatively or at the same time. Singers tend to mix it up quite a lot, but for teachers, it is healthier to breathe by your nose because it filters and warms up the air before it goes down to your lungs. This will prevent your vocal cords from drying out too quickly, especially in air-conditioned environments. It is also a good way to pace your voice by slowing down your speech rhythm and taking the time to breathe properly. You don't have to fill your lungs to their full capacity as long as you take the sufficient amount of air to sustain each speaking line. What is essential, though, is to breathe naturally and quietly with no muscle restriction. That includes letting your belly in and out just like a sleeping baby would.

Ready for some homework? Time to practice correct deep breathing. Lie down to the ground with a book on your belly. Watch it raise and come down as you breathe. It goes up when you breathe in and it goes down as you exhale. If the book stays immobile, that means you are only filling up the top part of your lungs. It is important not to force the stomach out but to let it come out naturally powered by the breath.

Make sure you don't waste the chance to master your breathing potential at every opportunity possible. Practicing deep breathing in your bed when you wake up in the morning or at night before going to sleep is an excellent strategy to energize yourself for another hard working school day or help rid your mind of unnecessary stress as your day comes to end.

Deep breathing lying down is one thing, but doing the same standing up is much more difficult. For that reason, practice deep breathing standing up straight as well. First, make sure you have the correct posture. The easiest way to make sure your posture is correct is as follows: Stand with your feet side by side, about shoulder width apart. Slightly lean forward on the balls of your feet. Push your breastbone out (the long flat bone in the center of your chest) and stand up straight; you are Mr. or Ms. Confidence!

Next, inhale slowly but quietly still through your nose, letting the air seem as if it is filling the bottom of your abdomen without allowing your shoulders to rise. If your shoulders move up, you are only filling the upper portion of your lungs. In fact, you are only using 1/3 of your breath capacity. The same applies if your thorax (mid-upper chest) expands but your belly doesn't.

Again, let your stomach come out without pushing it out. This motion must take its course naturally. If it feels uncomfortable, you're doing it wrong. To prevent your shoulders and upper body from rising, you can raise up your arms as you inhale and let them go down as you exhale. It should do the trick. Watch yourself breathe in front of a mirror to make sure you are doing it properly. Your belly should expand first, then your front and back ribs, followed by your chest. Let everything go when you exhale. Relax! Now try once more. I have to say this again: remember to breathe quietly and let your belly out as the air is coming in. You might feel hesitant about not tucking in your belly but it is a must. Keeping your belly in forces the upper part of your body to lift your larynx and squeeze your vocal cords. Breathing loudly, is a sign of larynx tension and airways restriction. Both must be avoided. Absolutely avoided!

A great imagery technique to help you concentrate on deep breathing is to pretend to smell the perfume of a beautiful flower. Let its fragrance open up your sinuses and lead the airflow to your lungs at the same time. You might feel a little dizzy if you're not used to slow breathing that way but don't worry; it's completely normal! After a while, the dizziness will go away. Just don't practice while driving! If you do become dizzy, sit down and take a break. Try again when you're ready.

Now that you can breathe deeply properly, let's try to make better use of your support by engaging your diaphragm. This is called diaphragmatic breathing. The diaphragm has a crucial function in breathing; it helps to regulate how much pressure is used to let the air in and out of your lungs. It expands during inhalation to suck the air in. During exhalation, it normally comes back up but what we want to do here is keep it expanded as long as possible to slowly control how much air is let out. Inhale deeply like you did before but exhale through your mouth slowly as if you were blowing candles on a birthday cake.

Put both hands on your hips slightly above your belly button with your thumbs feeling your lowest back ribs and all of your other fingers at the front. When you inhale, notice how your rib cage expands. Your thumbs might even feel like they are coming away from each other a little bit. Try to keep your front and back ribs expanded while you exhale. Your ribs will naturally want to sink in but try to fight the inward motion by applying a slight downward push. This abdominal pressure exercised by your front and back muscles should feel very similar to how they interact in the actions of blowing your nose, coughing or even going to the washroom! Never apply pressure by pushing your belly in because it will tighten your throat. Again, don't think forward and don't think inward. Think downward! Repeat this several times. If you need to further engage your diaphragm, bend your knees a bit in a sitting motion. You should apply a slight downward pressure as you exhale and especially if you're about to speak loudly. The louder the voice, the better the push, but never to the extent that it's making you feel uncomfortable.

I know all of this might sound a little complicated but since a picture is worth a thousand words, I thought I'd share with you the mental depiction I visualize to use my support properly. In essence, it is based on the imagery of my body as a giant syringe. If you're afraid of needles don't worry; it won't hurt! First, I visualize a giant syringe in my body. Second, I take a big breath and I imagine a round and flat platform at my belly button level. It feels like a wide ring or a tire pressing against the inside contour of my waist. Third, I start applying a downward pressure during exhalation or during speech and I visualize it slowly pressing down and against the syringe's cylinder (the inside contour of my waist) hence

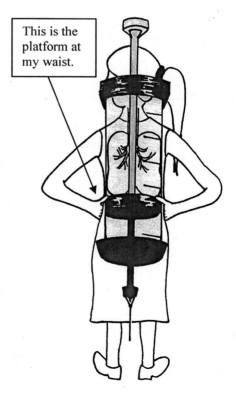

This is the platform at my waist.

preventing my ribs from collapsing and losing the expansion acquired during inhalation. I actually pretend that air is coming out of the syringe (rather than from my mouth). Finally, I resist letting the platform come back up. I continue pressing down for as long as I can or until it feels like the platform has reached the bottom of the syringe and I'm out of air. Obviously, we both know that the air is not coming out from down there but rather from the mouth! It almost feels like the downward pressure propels the air or the voice off the floor up in an opposite force. Just like a rocket launch!

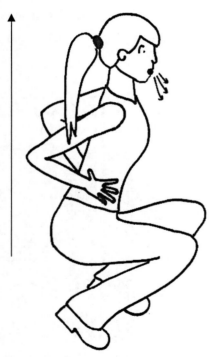

A good exercise to develop resistance against the temptation of pulling your stomach in or letting your diaphragm come up rather than applying a downward pressure during exhalation and keep your ribs expanded is to do squats. Start by standing up straight and pull your shoulders back as discussed above, with both hands above your hips. Place your feet shoulder length apart. Inhale and descend, keeping your knees in line with your feet. Keep your back straight and never look down. Descend until you have a 90-degree angle to the ground. Come back to a standing position without bouncing at the bottom. Exhale at the same time, focusing on your downward pressure as if you were propelling yourself from the ground and keep your ribs expanded as long as you can. Synchronizing the squats with your breathing is integral to the success of this exercise. I recommend visualizing the syringe imagery during the ascent and exhalation to help you apply better muscle resistance and achieve the goal of proper breath management and, most importantly, support control. Repeat a dozen times daily.

There is another excellent breathing exercise that helps engaging the diaphragm. It is called "The Stuttering Snake". I always use this exercise as part of my vocal warm-up when I teach choir at my school. Kids love it (and you will, too)! Take a deep breath in and exhale on a hiss. Repeat a few times before you try again but next time, quickly break off the hissing in short rhythmic sounds. If you put your hands around your waist as described earlier, you will feel your diaphragm moving back and forth as you apply the downward pressure to maintain the broken hiss. Good job!

RELAXING THE TONGUE AND LARYNX
The next exercise will help you relax your face, tongue and jaw to let your larynx get into position on its own. Most people generally don't have too many problems with that in their speaking voice. Tongue tension and the raising of the larynx are more frequent during singing due to more variances in pitch.

To help release tension in your tongue and larynx, try the following relaxation exercise: Yawn. Then do it again. Yawn once more. Doing the arm action helps! Raise the arms up like when yawning. Hey, don't be shy... Nobody's watching, haha! There you go; your jaw and tongue are now both completely relaxed. That is what you aim for during speech and especially while you sing and move up and down through your register. Let's try again without actually yawning this time. Open your mouth as if you were about to yawn, breathing through your nose and mouth at the same time if you can. This is often referred to as the yawning sensation. Don't let your tongue fall in the back of your throat. Its tip should slightly rest on top of your front lower teeth or behind them. Don't plant the tongue there, just let it be.

When your tongue is totally relaxed, you will notice it will come into the shape of a "u" in the back of your throat. The yawning will help you relax the tongue down into the "u" shape. Look in a mirror to see if it's good or not. It's important not to try manipulating the tongue into the "u" shape or it won't work! It can only happen through relaxation. Sometimes people make the mistake of trying so hard that they create tension instead of letting the tongue relax naturally, which defies our purpose here. If one side of your tongue is higher than the other, then your tongue is tensed. If it wiggles from side to side, it's another sign of tension as well. Just let the "u" occur as naturally as possible. Yawn again and again if you have to. Louder. Louder! Yawning is contagious; I want to yawn as well now... You did good!

The tongue should always more or less go back to that position during enunciation. If it goes backward too much, its base crushes the vocal cords. If it goes forward too much, it lifts the front of the larynx excessively and places inadequate tension on the vocal cords. Pretend to yawn once more and hold the yawning position for a couple seconds. Then, count aloud from one to ten, always reverting to that relaxed neutral position between each number.

Another way to get this area of your face to relax is to say "huh" or "haw" as if you learned new information that surprised you. I got this idea after reading an article in the Canadian magazine *MacLean's*[11] about teaching immigrants how to lose

---

[11] Lunau, Kate. "Removing the Accent from Success: An American Helps Immigrants Lose their Accent". Maclean's. July 2nd, 2007. Maclean's Magazine. October 10th, 2010 <http://www.macleans.ca/article.jsp?content=20070702_107049_107049>

their foreign accents. That's how the author Kate Lunau got her students to relax their tongue. It made me realize how worked up we sometimes get when we teach. If I'm not careful, I know I sometimes feel tension in my tongue and jaw at the end of a lesson and I know that affects my voice negatively. So beware! You can practice saying "huh" following it by a count of one to ten: "huh" one, "huh" two, et cetera. Do the same with yawns: "yawn" one, "yawn" two, et cetera.

Here is another suggestion to help you achieve the "u" position in the back of your tongue and relax it completely. Breathe by the nose with the tip of your tongue touching the very front of your palate, right by your upper teeth. Let the tongue fall down naturally as you exhale. You can even yawn it down if you want to. Pull the tip of the tongue back up against your upper gum when you inhale again, then let it fall during exhalation. Repeat the same exercise but this time say "la" with a strong "l" as you exhale. The way your tongue falls into position on "la" is exactly how it should sit between articulations. Once again as a next step, you can alternate "la" with numbers one to ten.

You will notice that yawning and saying "huh" help the jaw relax and open wide vertically as opposed to horizontally. Place your fingers at the end of your jaw line just below your earlobes. You will feel the tip of your jawbone back up when you open wide with the yawn sensation or "huh". It's a good indication that the larynx has tilted and is in position to let your vocal cords vibrate effortlessly. Maintaining that position during speech is unrealistic but do try to open your mouth that way before addressing your class loudly and, most importantly, during elocution on words with open vowels whenever it is possible, for example, "Guys!", "Stop!", "Quiet!".

If you feel tension in your face around your cheeks, gently press with the palms of your hands underneath your cheekbones to release it. Relaxing your tongue, jaw and face while you talk helps tilt your larynx and elongate the vocal cords sufficiently in order to vibrate freely.

NATURAL RESONATORS

Your body is your instrument when it comes to projecting your voice. There are three main areas of focus where the voice resonates: your chest, your throat and your head. A trained singer will cleverly direct his or her voice into its resonators to create a balanced sound without hurting his or her vocal cords. I want you to be as resourceful as possible when it comes to using your speaking voice. Instinctively, the lower the voice, the lower we tend to direct it towards its lowest resonance area: the chest. It is not surprising that similarly the higher the sound, the higher we tend to direct it towards its highest resonance area: the head. Both extremes will generate unnecessary strain on an untrained voice unless the larynx is relaxed completely even though it is also possible to speak in a medium-pitched voice (not too high and not too low) and improperly direct the sound in the throat and chest alone. That, too, is unhealthy. Why is the voice often so challenging when placed in the chest and throat? Simply because balancing the larynx forward and elongating the vocal cords properly while maintaining a state of relaxation is not always easy. A trained singer is taught to engage the larynx properly and focus the voice to balance the resonance and avoid damage. My goal is not to make you a singer. Instead, I want to teach you where to place your voice so your larynx relaxes and tilts logically in place and offers your vocal cords an ideal environment to vibrate freely. All of that has to occur naturally because I'm sure all this larynx-tilting jargon is going way over your head!

What you need to know is that directing your voice towards the head resonators while mixing it in with a little bit of chest resonance is a must. The goal is to resonate the entire body with a balanced sound. It will provide your vocal cords with enough length and room to vibrate in a healthy manner. Moreover, it will allow your voice to project effortlessly. You could compare not using your head resonators to filling one side of an acoustic guitar's body with a towel. The sound would obviously not be as loud unless it can vibrate to its full potential. I will soon teach you how to give your voice as much room as possible to resonate. You will hear the results immediately: your voice will be louder without sounding harsh.

Before we go any further, I would like you to try the following experiment to find out how you can make your voice travel in your head and ultimately down to your throat and chest to discover the different areas of resonance in your body. This will give you a better understanding of your core resonators. The following exercises will help you to find your natural voice.

EXERCISE #1A: MAKE YOUR SOUND TRAVEL

First, speak with your voice completely in your nose; just like a witch or a duck. Take the witch "ah, ah, ah" for example. Pinch your nose. If your tone changes, it is proof that your voice is completely focused in your nose and it should sound very nasal! Now, move the vibrations and the focus of your voice up a tiny bit as if it were sitting ON rather than IN your nose. If you can pinch (and release) your nostrils without hearing the sound of your voice being altered and becoming nasal, congratulations! You have the right placement for your voice and it is properly balanced.

Hold that sound on "ah" for a moment. You should feel a lot of resonance in your head when your voice is focused that way. There should also be a lot of buzzing happening all around your nose. Lots of resonance and buzzing is the sensation you are looking for. Close your eyes and hold that sound again for a moment. Feel and listen to your voice vibrating in this area of your face. I will come back to that placement later and teach you different ways to get there, but for now, keep moving your voice further up around your forehead and then make it sit on top your head. Close your eyes and hold that sound for a moment. Feel and listen again to your voice. Since you are getting slightly away from the ideal placement, the resonance and buzzing should not only have moved a little but it should also have decreased a bit as well.

Now, let your voice slide down towards the back of your head until it reaches the area between your ears. Close your eyes and hold that sound still on "ah" for a moment. Feel and listen again to your voice. The resonance and buzzing should still be happening but notice how the focus is different around your ear canals. Now, direct it down your neck, in your throat and as low as possible around your chest. When you focus your voice in the chest, a lot of vibrations occur around your neck and upper-body. This gives a false impression of loudness. Remember that this placement doesn't allow your larynx to pull your vocal cords properly when you speak with a medium pitch, not too low and not too high in your register. That is why we want to stay away from the chest voice; but it is good for you to know what all these different placements feel and sound like so you can stay away or aim for them. Finally, bring your voice back up in your nose where you started. See the following illustration for a visual reference:

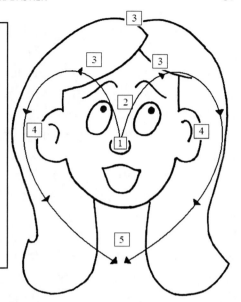

Make Your Sound Travel

1) Nasal voice

2) ON rather than IN your nose

3) Around your forehead and on top of your head

4) Back of your head and between your ears

5) In your throat

It might be difficult to feel where the voice resonates the first time you try this exercise. Don't worry if you don't get it right on your first try. This is the perfect example of why the voice is intricate and a challenging instrument "to play". You cannot use your hands to manipulate the sound or your eyes to see what you are trying to do. In order to move the focus of your voice, you will need to use your mind. Visualize where you want your voice to be in your body. You will also need to rely on the sensations that come from the voice vibrating in certain resonance chambers of your chest and head. Imagine a water fountain in your body. Suppose that your diaphragm, your support, jets water into your head. Then, visualize a ping-pong ball floating on top of the jet. The water jet helps to keep your support connected with your voice. The ping-pong ball is your point of focus and it is what you want to send in different resonance chambers: the nose, the forehead, the back of your head and your throat. You can even imagine the ping-pong ball moving faster and faster as the vibrations become stronger.

This simple imagery should help you connect your support to your voice and propel it confidently where you want it to go.

As you can see, the head alone is a wonderful space for your voice to resonate. I want to take you back to where I congratulated you for finding the right placement of your voice. This facial area is commonly known as "the mask". This is a term that has gained popularity in the Italian tradition of Bel Canto (beautiful singing). The expression "the mask" comes from the renaissance period when men and women wore costumes and fancy masks to masquerade balls in Europe. These masks generally covered the area of the face where we want voice vibrations to be focused. The mask covers the sinus cavities around your nose and cheeks, between your eyes, and on your forehead. You will be happy to know that these are largely accountable for creating your own beautiful and distinctive tone and color. There is therefore no coincidence in the name Bel Canto being attributed to focusing the voice in that area!

Speaking in the mask implies directing the vibrations of your voice in your sinus cavities rather than in your nose. You can easily imagine the mask based on where the sinus cavities are located in the face.

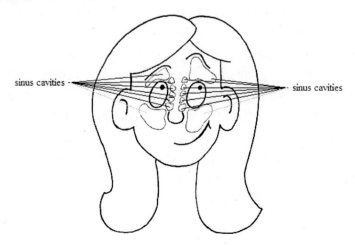

The difficulty is to stay away from a nasal tone even though it is an excellent starting point to find your correct voice placement. Try this exercise again (start with a nasal voice and move it until it feels as if it is sitting ON your nose and hold the sound once pinching your nostrils doesn't affect the tone anymore), but this time practice saying your alphabet when you have found your correct placement. Whenever you are concerned that you might sound nasal, just pinch your nose again for a quick and easy checkup!

EXERCISE #2: LEANING FORWARD

With this exercise, you will be able to send your voice into the mask really easily with little effort. Grab today's newspaper or any reading material handy, lean forward and start reading it out loud. Bend forward to a comfortable level until your head is hanging down. Thanks to the laws of gravity, your voice will naturally fall in the right spot. Keep reading and pay special attention once again to where the buzzing occurs, how the voice resonates, and consequently, what it sounds like. Now, keep reading and slowly straighten up without moving the focus of your voice. That is very important. Continue to feel the buzzing and resonance in the upper forward area of your face: the mask. Listen to the sound of your tone and maintain it. If you lost your placement straightening up, lean forward again and try once more! Listen carefully to your voice again to preserve the same quality when you rise.

EXERCISE #3: PUSHING YOUR BREASTBONE

This one is fairly simple as well. It doesn't matter if you're sitting down or standing up. Make a fist with one hand and grasp it with the other. Place them both on your breastbone (the middle of your chest). Hold a note on "ah" or any other vowel you wish; it doesn't really matter. You don't have to worry about placing the sound properly at this point because the next maneuver will just do that for you! Press quickly but firmly (not too forcefully; this is not a

cardiac massage!) against your breastbone. You should feel your resonance being thrown up into the mask right at this moment. It will only last momentarily until your voice falls back to its original placement so you have to try a few times in a row to get a real feel of where this brings your voice to. What's important is that pressing your breastbone will throw your voice into the mask regardless of where it originated. This is where you want to aim your voice all the time. Let's bring this a little further. The next step is to hold a note as loud as possible and beat your chest one fist at a time very quickly. Gotcha! Tarzan is in the house, haha!

EXERCISE #4: STICK YOUR TONGUE OUT!

It is practically impossible to speak in your throat when sticking the tongue out because it forces the lower jaw to collapse, the larynx to tilt forward and it sends the resonance of the voice right up there, where it belongs. Stick your tongue out and say "ah" to get a good sense of where the buzzing should be happening: around your nose, forehead and cheeks. Yes, the mask! This is all that this exercise consists of: sticking your tongue out and holding an "ah" or other vowels for a few seconds. Try to become aware of what it feels like for the voice to resonate in the mask. It is primarily its purpose although it is also useful to release unwanted tension in the tongue.

EXERCISE #5: PITCHING ABOVE THE PENCIL

There are different ways to get your voice in the mask. It's neat to try different techniques to see what works best for you. Melissa Cross created another exercise that I find quite successful. She is a renowned vocal coach for extreme vocals and creator of *The Zen of Screaming*.[12] I like this exercise because using a pencil seems quite appropriate in the classroom!

Place a clean pencil (or a straw) horizontally in your mouth. Say "ah" while trying to pitch the sound of your voice above the pencil. Compare how different your voice sounds when you try pitching under the pencil. Notice as well how your larynx tends to tilt forward, raising its back and lowering its front to elongate the vocal cords.

EXERCISE #6: BRRR

You will need to use more drama skills for this exercise. Let's start! First, close your eyes. Imagine yourself standing outside on a winter night. Snow is softly falling. It's a beautiful evening, but there is one problem: you forgot to wear a jacket! Now, pretend that you are cold, very cold. All of a sudden, your body

---

[12] Cross, Melissa. The Zen of Screaming: Vocal Instruction For A New Breed. MMV Loudmouth Inc. February 21st, 2007.

starts shivering. Feel goose bumps appearing all over your skin and say "brrr" expressively as you act that out. Do it once again but this time, listen carefully to the pitch on which you say "brrr". That is the correct pitch for your natural dynamic voice. Repeat one last time and add, "I'm so cold!"

The sound "brrr" should naturally bring your voice forward into the mask. We are looking for a very buzzing "brrr", not a throaty or breathy "brrr" of course. Hopefully you were able to keep your resonance up there when you said, "I'm so cold!" You can try this exercise again substituting "I'm so cold!" by "My name is ____", "I'm ____ years old!", "I have ____ children", et cetera. Don't forget to start with "brrr"!

EXERCISE #7: UMM-HMMM

I'd like to borrow Dr. Morton Cooper's exercise from his book *Change Your Voice, Change Your Life* to help you find your natural dynamic speaking voice. It simply is one of the most efficient speaking voice placement exercises I have come across. It works wonders. *Say "umm-hmmm," using rising inflection with the lips closed. It is vital that this "umm-hmmm" be spontaneous and sincere.*[13] In order to do this, positively answer the following questions with "umm-hmmm" (you must agree!):

- Do you enjoy teaching?
- Are you a great teacher?
- Are you proud of your students?
- Isn't teaching the most wonderful profession of all?

At this point, you must listen to the pitch on which you are answering "umm-hmmm".

---

[13] Cooper, Dr Morton. Change Your Voice, Change Your Life. New York, NY. Macmillan, 1984, p. 23

- Will you feel relieved when your report cards will be done?
- Are you looking forward to your next vacation?

The pitch produced by this exercise is the one at which you should be speaking at all times. Not so much lower, not so much higher, but approximately at that same mid tone level. The second part of the exercise requires you to count from 1 to 10 saying "umm-hmmm" in front of each number and on the same pitch: "Umm-hmmm" one, "umm-hmmm" two, "umm-hmmm" three, and so on.

Continue practicing your correct pitch and placement by saying "umm-hmmm" in front of sentences you often repeat in your classroom. For example:

- Umm-hmmm. Get in line, everybody!
- Umm-hmmm. Time to tidy up!
- Umm-hmmm. Time for recess!

I've taught several of my colleagues how to find their natural dynamic speaking voice using this technique during a workshop at my school. Here is a funny story from my friend and teacher Robyn Benjamin (Toronto, ON) after she tried it for herself:

"After listening to Valerie's suggestion of saying "umm-hmmm" to find your head voice, I decided to try and use this strategy while reading my students a book. I found myself saying "umm-hmmm" after every couple of sentences to ensure that I was using my head voice. I didn't realize just how frequently I was saying "umm-hmmm" until I noticed that a couple of my students in the front row decided to say 'umm-hmmm' with me!

Now, I try and say 'umm-hmmm' and a few words before the students enter the library. Overall, I find this technique to be quite effective at saving my throat."

EXERCISE #8 : HAVE A GOOD LAUGH!

Laughter is a feel-good activity with numerous therapeutic effects. According to John-Ryan of www.jokes-comedy.com, *"a good joke may lower the blood pressure, improve memory and cognitive functions and boost the immune system. Moreover, these results are not short-term only: it seems that a good sense of humor may protect you against heart diseases and alter your biochemical state to a level where the organism produces more antibodies."*[14] The reason I brought this up is that laughing will automatically direct the vibrations of your voice into the mask. Take a couple minutes to laugh. Listen and feel where the resonance is concentrated. A good hearty laugh will be physically felt in the soft palate, which is perfect to guide you towards finding your natural dynamic voice. Try the following exercise:

1) Stand up straight.

2) Breathe deeply.

3) Pretend to laugh as naturally as possible on the vowel "a" as in "ah, ah, ah!" If this is difficult, you can also try to mimic Santa Claus' laugh on "o" as in "ho, ho, ho!"

4) Listen carefully to the sound of your voice and try to feel where the sound places itself. Hopefully, you will feel something happening around your soft palate, and your nose and cheek area—all around your sinuses. The voice should be placed in the mask as discussed earlier.

---

[14] Ryan, John. "How Laughing is Good for your Health". A World of Good Health. October 10th, 2010. <http://www.aworldofgoodhealth.com/articles/laughter-for-health.htm>

Laughing also engages your diaphragm and encourages correct support and breath management.

5) Breathe in and laugh again!

You can also count, say your alphabet, or simple sentences while laughing before each. After all this hard work, I hope laughing that much has helped you relax a little as well!

PRACTICE, PRACTICE AND PRACTICE SOME MORE!
Practice these exercises daily until you feel comfortable with the new placement of your natural dynamic voice. Before the morning bell, during recess if you're off duty, during lunchtime, after school, or before going to bed! With time, finding the right placement for your speaking voice will become easier. You can even practice during class just like Ms. Benjamin did. I love it when people get creative and her story really put a smile on my face that day.

Another teacher also told me minutes before attending another of my workshops that when she told her class she was going to learn about how to use her speaking voice properly, all of her students wanted her to report back to them and teach them how to do it as well because they too often lose their voice. So why not make it a fun class activity once in a while? I know I have! Effective voice habits can be taught to children at an early age and save thousand of voices. I have prepared a lesson plan to include all of the exercises above with their highlights at the end of this book for you and your students. It can be done in its entirety during a drama and dance lesson or broken up in shorter episodes. These vocal exercises are also excellent to prepare the voice during music class. They are fun and kid appropriate. Simply, they are perfect when your students need a break to move a little and take their mind off work for a few seconds. Either way, they will get a kick out of it!

I guarantee that the more you practice, the faster you will build muscle memory and tear down any previous incorrect vocal habits. If you come to a point where you feel like it's just not happening, don't give up. Stop, breathe deeply and detach yourself from the process. Take a break and do something else for a while—why not get ahead on your grading? Don't pressure yourself. It's better to stop rather than repeat errors. Then, come back to it a few minutes later—or the next day if you have to wait that long. Congratulate yourself: Fantastic job! Keep it up!

CHAPTER NINE
Raising Your Voice

As you know from an earlier chapter, a common problem with the speaking voice is to use a pitch that is lower than the natural speaking voice. That often happens to (unconsciously) show control or after a cold. In order to find your natural dynamic speaking voice, you might have to raise the pitch of your voice a bit and speak a little higher to enable your larynx to find its natural comfortable neutral position. Only then, can the rest of the vocal apparatus maintain relaxation during speech.

By no means do I intend to say that you can never speak with a low-pitched voice. However, it is generally more difficult to keep the larynx from shifting up and down and contract during speech fluctuation if your voice is too low to start with. The same applies if your voice is too high. After you've adjusted that, you want to be able to raise the intensity of your voice without hurting your vocal cords in order to project the voice over the classroom noise. That leads us to the next paragraph.

PLACEMENT VERSUS INTENSITY
As discussed earlier, your natural dynamic speaking voice should sit somewhere in the middle of your range. There are different voice definitions that are important for you to know to understand better how to use your voice. These fall into two categories: placement and intensity.

VOICE PLACEMENT
Voice placement refers to where in your body your voice naturally resonates. Imagine that your whole body can resonate

like a tuning fork. You can decide where you want it to resonate the most to keep your vocal cords safe from injury. The rule is simple: the lower you go into your range, the more vibrations will naturally be felt more strongly in your chest. We call this type of voice "chest voice". On the other hand, the higher you go in your range, vibrations will naturally be felt more strongly in your head. We call this type of voice "head voice". Voice fatigue is often caused by using a pitch that should naturally vibrate into head voice but instead is focused in chest voice. There is nothing wrong with the chest voice in itself as long as the larynx remains 100% relaxed during speech; and that is sometimes difficult to do. The voice becomes uncomfortable when the larynx cannot enlarge and tilt back and forth to elongate the cords properly and instead raises without the stretch and necessary angle required, and thereby preventing the cords from vibrating freely. When the vocal cords lack the room they need to vibrate, that is when damage occurs.

INTENSITY

Voice intensity refers to the amount of vibrations you put into your voice and therefore how much your body resonates from it. There are three different intensity levels to rely on: soft, medium and loud.

The soft voice uses little effort to project and is at a low

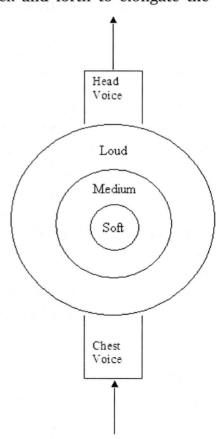

volume. It is smooth and sweet and can therefore be used on any pitch. For a teacher, a soft voice would be most appropriate when working one-on-one with a student. Use a soft voice to discuss delicate matters such as pointing out mistakes or discussing an emotionally charged topic that would otherwise make the student uncomfortable such as family issues or social skills. It is naturally nurturing and calming.

The medium voice is a standard volume voice that is ideal during direct teaching. It's simple: the class should be quiet enough that you can be heard without having to be loud. It is very close to your natural intensity. This is how loud you would normally speak when interacting in a group, whether it is with colleagues, friends or kids.

As for the loud voice, it is the intensity that requires the most careful attention. To project your voice loudly over a group of kids, you will have to place the resonance of your voice into its resonators, the mask, and use your diaphragm to support and propel it across the room properly according to the principles described earlier on in this book! A loud voice will be most useful to call upon students during transition periods, to cheer kids during gym or at a game, to ask the class to line up or tidy up, et cetera.

TONE COLORS

Other singing terminologies widely in use in the vocal field are the descriptive "Falsetto" and "Full Voice". The first term, falsetto, is well known and often used to describe a breathy high-pitched male voice. It is possible for both males and females to speak and sing using falsetto. Because of its breathy quality, I would recommend not using it too much as it can dry out the vocal cords over time. Instead, I would encourage you to use your full voice, which is your natural voice. The full voice is of outmost interest to us thanks to its rich tone and colorful quality. In full voice, one can speak or sing effortlessly. It is vibrant and energizing. It feels alive. It is your natural dynamic speaking or singing voice. The voice you have been working on since you started reading this book. The voice that is beautiful and free!

HOW DO THEY WORK TOGETHER?

It is a good idea to be able to measure the intensity at which you speak, where the voice is placed and the type of voice to use that is the most appropriate for you in order to have better control on what pitch to speak and at which volume by making it a conscious decision. This will be easier done if you speak using the beginning of your head voice—let's call that the low head voice—because your larynx will be in a neutral position and your resonance most likely focused in the mask. However, even though your focus is low in head voice, some resonance will overflow in your chest. It becomes a bit of a mixture between the head and chest voice. A more official terminology for it would be the "Mixed Voice".

There are many benefits in maintaining your low head voice or mixed voice while you talk. Again, you might have to raise the pitch of your voice a little to find your low head voice and let it vibrate in your natural resonators. If you find that your natural pitch, the one you found with Dr. Morton Cooper's "Umm-hmmm" exercise described in the previous chapter, for example, is already close to the pitch you were already speaking with, then don't raise it. It might just be a matter of refocusing your resonance in the mask. Don't raise your pitch unreasonably or your larynx might unnecessarily start to raise and tense your throat, creating problems. The point is that you want to be able to speak over noise without hurting your vocal cords. Focusing the vibrations of your voice forward into that area while keeping your larynx completely relaxed and engaging your diaphragm to support your voice does just that by taking away most of the pressure from your vocal cords. It gives your speaking voice an incomparable dynamic, allowing you to project it better. It's that simple.

Raising your voice and using your natural pitch will give you a pleasant tone. It will beautify your voice and make people more interested in what you have to say because it's in us to praise beauty. It will naturally convey positivism, which is also something people want to relate to; just like smiling and laughing, the latter being an extension of your voice. By the way, most people laugh using a higher voice—people are happy when they laugh! Think about it: we all aspire to be happy and happiness is contagious.

Once you have found the right pitch for your voice, your larynx will naturally open up to sit comfortably in your throat, preventing your vocal cords from rubbing each other and creating damage during speech.

I cannot emphasize this enough! It will most likely reflect in your confidence and in your ability to manage your class as well. Your students will pay more attention to what you teach and they will become better listeners. When you discipline your students with your new voice, they will listen better to what you have to say because your tone won't irritate them further by translating into anger. This is where authentic communication begins. You will sound composed and calm. Symptoms of vocal exhaustion will disappear, and as a result, your physical health and moods will improve. People will perceive you as a happier person, and you will feel less stressed out and so much better about yourself at the end of the day.

IT DOESN'T SOUND LIKE ME!

You might not be used to your new sound, so give yourself some time to get accustomed to it. I can assure you that you don't sound funny or weird, but you sound lovely and in control. Just like the author of *Effortless Mastery*, Kenny Werner writes in his book that to overcome your own barriers a little bit of self-brainwashing may be necessary here!   Keep repeating to yourself: *"That is the most beautiful sound I have ever heard!"*[15] Say it again! I promise you that after a little while, you will feel so content about your new voice that you will never, ever want to go back to the old one again. You can do it!

---

[15] Werner, Kenny. Effortless Mastery. New Albany, IN. Jamey Aebersold Jazz, Inc., 1996, p. 91

CHAPTER TEN
Daily Voice Warm-Up

In order to help you start your day on a positive note, I highly recommend that you arrive to school approximately a half-hour early to warm-up your voice, especially at the beginning while you are trying to get accustomed to your new voice and sustain it throughout the day. Warming-up will slightly raise your body temperature, which increases the flexibility of the muscles and cartilages involved in the speech process. It will also bring back your muscle memory and enhance your correct placement. You are not only a teacher; you're an athlete!

Always start with a quick 5-10 minute stretch. Do a couple of neck rolls, shoulder rolls, arm circles, torso twists, et cetera. Massage your neck and trapezium muscles (the long muscles on each sides of your neck that extend to your shoulder blades). I must say that I particularly enjoy the forward bend, which you can do seated or standing. It provides a complete stretch of the neck, spine, legs and even the arms depending on the effort of your pull but remember not to lock your knees as that can be harmful. The forward bend even relaxes the digestive system apparently. During the forward bend, let each breath expand your lungs. If you hold your breath while bending down, you can feel the air push against the walls of your ribs. The muscles surrounding your respiratory system are core components of voice production so get your voice box muscles to work! Now, are you ready for some vocal gymnastics?

WARM-UP #1: DEEP BREATHING

This is similar to what you have learned about breathing properly.

a) Stand up straight. Watch your posture. Inhale slowly and quietly through your nose, letting the air fill the bottom of your abdomen without allowing your shoulders to rise. Stay relaxed.

b) Raise your arms as you inhale and let them go down as you exhale to prevent your shoulders and upper body from rising. Let your belly come out naturally at all times.

c) Repeat five times. Remember that you might feel a little dizzy if you're not used to breathing that way, but don't worry; it's normal! If this happens, sit down, take a break and try again when you're ready.

WARM-UP #2: CONSONANTS THAT ARE GOOD FOR YOUR BELLY!

Here are a few consonants that will help you develop a strong natural support for your voice.

a) Take a deep quiet breath. Watch your posture; stand up straight! Stay relaxed.

a) Exhale on "sss".

b) Repeat five times.

c) Inhale slowly again, and then exhale on "ffff".

d) Repeat five times.

e) Continue breathing deeply, and as you exhale, switch to "vvv" on any pitch of your choice. You can pretend that you're starting your car's engine if that helps!

f) Try the same warm-up exercises with "zzz". Feel the vibrations of your voice in the mask.

g) One variation of this exercise is to pause often to cut off the sound without breathing in until you're out of breath. For example: "sss", pause, "sss", pause, et cetera. As you'll recall, this is called the Stuttering Snake! You can do this at a slow or fast pace as you wish. Another variation is to maintain the sound but change the intensity from soft to loud. On "sss" for example, increase, then decrease the volume/energy on one breath. The soft versus loud continuation evokes the sound of the wind.

WARM-UP #3: WATER GARGLE

Athletes constantly drink water to keep their body hydrated. Likewise, your water intake will keep your vocal cords lubricated. The next warm-up exercise works your breath endurance, support, voice placement and massages your vocal cords, providing them with hydration.

a) Take a little bit of water in your mouth. Don't drink it! Close your mouth.

b) Breathe deeply through your nose. Watch your posture; stand up straight! Stay relaxed.

c) Lean your head backward, open your mouth and gargle as long as you can. You will last longer if you're using your support correctly.

d) Be careful not to let your tongue fall in the back of your throat or it will move the placement of your voice there as well.

e) Keep the tip of your tongue slightly on top of or behind your front lower teeth.

f) Send the vibrations of your voice in the mask.

g) Repeat five times. Count how long you last so you can compare your breath endurance and support control between each try.

WARM-UP #4: LIP BUBBLES

This one is a lot of fun and known worldwide for its effectiveness. Most singers use lip bubbles to warm-up their voice and place it in the mask therefore so should you!

a) Seal you lips together.

b) Take a deep quiet breath through your nose. Stand up straight! Stay relaxed.

c) Allow the air to steadily flow out of your mouth using your support to produce a sound and let your lips vibrate. Start in the middle of your range. Then, slide down to the very bottom. You can make your pitch go up and down all you want! It takes a considerable amount of air pressure to achieve this. You should feel your diaphragm pulling down and a buzzing sensation on and around your lips and the front of your face.

d) Remember to keep the tip of your tongue forward slightly on top of or behind your front lower teeth.

e) Feel the vibrations of your voice in the mask. Avoid any breathiness in the sound. Focus instead on producing a crisp vibrant sound.

f) Your lips must remain absolutely relaxed to be able to pull this off. If you're not successful, it means your lips are too tensed. Relax!

g) Repeat five times.

WARM-UP #5: LIP BUBBLE VARIATIONS

These exercises start the same way as the one above except that you will break them down to allow your speaking voice to be heard on a specific sound or vowel.

a) Seal you lips together.

b) Take a deep quiet breath through your nose. Watch your posture and stay relaxed.

c) Choose a pitch in the middle of your range. Allow the air to flow out of your mouth using your support to produce a sound and let your lips vibrate on that pitch.

d) Open your mouth on the sound "ah".

e) From that pitch, slide down to the bottom of your range still on "ah".

f) Feel the vibrations of your voice in the mask.

g) Repeat five times.

h) You can do the same exercise starting at the bottom of your range with the lip bubbles. Slide up, then open your mouth at the top on "ah" and slide back down still on "ah". The degree of difficulty is much increased with this variation. Only try it when you feel completely confident with the straight lip bubble/"ah" exercise.

i) You can do the same exercise starting at the top of your range with the lip bubbles then opening your mouth at the bottom and slide back up on "ah". Most people will find that sliding up is more challenging than sliding down but please give it a try when you're ready.

j) Another variation is to choose different sounds to sing on. "Ah" and "eh" work particularly well. "Ih", "uh" and "oh" and closed vowels are a bit more challenging, but it's still good to practice them. If they pose a problem keeping the sound in the mask, attack the note on an easy, open vowel before going to the closed vowel: "ah-oh", "ah-ih", "eh-uh", et cetera.

WARM UP #6: TONGUE TRILLS

a) Inhale slowly and quietly through your nose while standing.

b) Bring the tip of your tongue forward behind your upper front teeth.

c) Push the air out of your mouth using your support to produce a sound on which to roll an Italian "r".

d) You can roll your "r" on any pitch. Raise the pitch up and down to cover your full range.

e) Feel the vibrations of your voice in the mask.

f) Repeat five times!

WARM-UP #7: THE VOCAL CORD STRETCH[16]

You are now ready to move on to producing a clean tone without the lip bubbles or tongue trills. This is one of my favorite exercises and it is also part of my good friend, mentor, and international vocal coach Jaime Vendera's Vocal Stress Release System warm-up program. I love it because it's easy and it really allows the vocal cords to loosen up. It is essentially a

---

[16] Vendera, Jaime. Raise Your Voice; Second Edition. Vendera Publishing, 2007, p. 235

singer's vocal exercise but anybody can do it, too! Basically, it consists of sliding up and down to cover one's entire vocal range.

a) Inhale slowly and quietly through your nose while standing. Stay relaxed.

b) Choose the vowel "eh" as in eggs, to start with and begin to sing on the lowest note of your register.

c) Raise the pitch of your voice to slide up to the highest note of your register.

d) Slide right back down to where you started.

e) Feel the vibrations of your voice in the mask.

f) Repeat 10 times on the same vowel (or different ones if you want) as long as you can maintain the richness and vibrant tones you found with "eh".

As Jaime explains in his book *Raise Your Voice Second Edition*, don't forget to keep the tone "clean and extremely resonant. The voice is shaped like a triangle. As you slide up in pitch (or ascend the scale), the tone will get thinner and pointier, and as you slide back down in pitch (descend), the tone will widen back out and become fuller. Keep the buzzing sensation on your teeth."[17]

WARM-UP #8: YOUR CLASSROOM LINGO

Here, you want to get accustomed to using your newfound natural dynamic speaking voice with sentences that are part of your daily speech routine. The emphasis really is to start creating brain and muscle memory around specific familiar vocabulary to keep you going on the right vocal path.

---

[17] Vendera, Jaime. Raise Your Voice: Second Edition. Vendera Publishing, 2007, p. 264

a) Write a list of the top ten sentences you repeat in your classroom:

1. _____

2. _____

3. _____

4. _____

5. _____

6. _____

7. _____

8. _____

9. _____

10. _____

b) While standing, breathe deeply and quietly. Stay relaxed.

c) Say "umm-hmmm" and follow with your first sentence. Be careful to say the sentence on the same pitch and with the same buzzing feel you got with the "umm-hmmm" and let it resonate in the mask.

d) Practice saying "umm-hmmm" in front of each sentence. Make sure that you are using your new natural dynamic speaking voice correctly.

e) Don't forget to engage your support.

Congratulations! You are done warming-up your voice. Well done! My last recommendation before you greet your students in the morning is to drink a large glass of water and drink some more throughout the day. If your throat feels dry, gargle water for immediate relief instead of drinking it. This will hydrate your vocal cords much faster then it would take your body to absorb the water and lubricate the cords. I am also including at the end of this book a lesson plan listing all of these exercises for your easy reference. Please feel free to take it up with your students the same way I suggested earlier with the Natural Dynamic Voice Placement Exercises lesson plan. I personally use a variety of these exercises to prepare my choir students to sing. You are ready; have a wonderful day!

PART THREE

Vocal Health

CHAPTER ELEVEN
Maintaining Your Voice

The vocal cords are sensitive parts of your body. Finding your natural dynamic speaking voice and being able to incorporate and apply the necessary vocal techniques into your daily vocal habits until it becomes second nature is the main factor in having a healthy voice. Other behaviors and daily activities also have either helpful or harmful repercussions on your vocal health. The next few tips encourage a positive lifestyle in accordance with maintaining your natural dynamic speaking voice and carrying you through your vocal journey.

DON'T . . .

DO NOT RAISE YOUR VOICE UNNECESSARILY
It sounds like a given but I had to mention it. Loud is not aloud! Always try to keep the volume of your voice at a natural level. Do not address your class until you have your students' full attention and they are as quiet as possible. I will share with you my ideas on how I do it in later chapters. Diversity is always something I look for in classroom management so hopefully that will give you some new and perhaps innovative ideas to take on your own.

DO NOT SMOKE
Another given! Cigarettes and smoke exposure greatly deteriorate the lining of the larynx and swell vocal cords. Very

serious voice-related diseases are attributed to smoking, including several forms of cancer. At the very least, smoking gives you bad breath and makes your hair and clothes smell terrible. It's also a very negative example for students. My mom used to smoke and I hated it as a child. I've always felt very strongly about a smoke free environment... Sorry!

DO NOT CLEAR YOUR THROAT

As hard as it can be, clearing your throat after coughing or if you feel like you have a frog in the throat will make the situation worse. The discomfort felt is caused by an over accumulation of mucus on the vocal cords. That can happen during a throat infection if you're not using your voice properly, or sometimes after meals. It can also be an early sign of vocal fatigue, so watch out for that.

In the first two cases, the body is trying to compensate for the irritation and is overreacting by producing too much mucus in an attempt to soothe the cords. Clearing the throat creates a friction between the vocal cords, aggravating the irritation further instead of helping it. It's a vicious circle. It might help to increase your water intake to lubricate your vocal cords better. Lip bubbles or any of the warm-up exercises you learned earlier are great at vibrating mucus away from your vocal cords gently with no harm induced. Other tips are to "suck on the inside of your lower lip, like sucking on a piece of hard candy"[18] or pretend blowing into a balloon to separate the cords and disintegrate the mucus. Other times, you just have to wait it out. This is what actually works best for me. It takes a lot of self-control, and the mucus feels annoying on my vocal cords for a little while but eventually, the irritation disappears and so do the mucus and the discomfort.

---

[18] Vendera, Jaime. Raise Your Voice; Second Edition. Vendera Publishing, 2007, p. 165

Some people might experience slight to severe acid reflux after meals that will be experienced with phlegm on the vocal cords and, in more serious cases, create lasting throat discomfort and irritation. Occasional acid reflux can be easily overturned with organic apple cider vinegar. By the way, if you're going to try this, I strongly recommend buying the Bragg's[19] brand. Whatever brand you buy, it needs to be organic; the one sitting on the shelves of your local grocery store does not work! Mix ½ a teaspoon of apple cider vinegar in a cup of water or juice and drink it half an hour before your meal or immediately after if your stomach starts acting up.

A few weeks ago, I had the misfortune of catching the stomach flu. I missed three days of work but I continued being ill for at least a week, always feeling bloated after my meals, et cetera. Then I noticed that after my meals, I always suffered from mucus on my vocal cords and my voice was becoming raspy. I think it might have been leftovers from the imbalance created in my stomach by the flu. I started using the apple cider vinegar before my meals and in a matter of a couple of days all was resolved! For persistent acid reflux, consult a doctor. You could be suffering from some food sensitivities or intolerances, some kind of stomach dysfunction, or weight might even have a role in your digestion. Medicine or other treatments could be necessary.

DO NOT DRINK COFFEE, TEA, ALCOHOL OR POP DRINKS

Yes, I know... This is a tough one! As much as I love these drinks, I had to stop. If you can't stop drinking coffee, for example, try at least to decrease how many you drink in a day. The reason behind this is that caffeine dehydrates your body and excites your glands, and it dries out the voice box. Your body

---

[19] "Bragg Apple Cider Vinegar", <u>Bragg Health Products and Books</u>. October 10th, 2010. <http://bragg.com/products/acv.html>

gets so much energy from caffeine that it overproduces phlegm to compensate for poorly hydrated vocal cords. That creates discomfort in your throat and makes you want to clear it more often, irritating it some more. It's another awful cycle. If you need that hot drink in the morning to start your day, why not try a ginger drink, cereal coffee or other coffee alternatives instead?

Ginger drinks are sold in most natural food stores and Chinese groceries. They're spicy and very soothing for the throat, especially if you're feeling under the weather! My grandmother used to drink cereal coffee every morning so I decided to give it a try this year. I bought a barley-based roasted drink that is supposed to taste similar to real coffee even though it definitely is not the same. It's an acquired taste, that's for sure. At first, I'd drink my barley coffee with a couple of cinnamon sticks to sweeten it and give it a more pleasant flavor but I eventually got used to the drink by itself. It's very filling and healthy, too. Just recently, my friend and colleague Jill Toombs, a vegan and the creator of Cakes by Jill[20] non-dairy ice cream cakes, told me about an amazing caffeine-free herbal coffee: Teeccino[21]. Jill always inspires me with her inventive recipes so for me, she is a highly trusted healthy food reference. The list of ingredients in Teeccino includes roasted carob, barley, chicory root, figs, dates and almonds. It is brewed like coffee and comes in a variety of different flavors. Actually, if you enjoy flavored coffee, Teeccino might be for you. I have yet to try them all; however, I have to say that I'm quite pleased with Java and Vanilla Nut. It's difficult to beat the real taste of coffee, particularly if you're a hardcore coffee lover, but take my word on this one: it tastes fantastic and I highly recommend it!

---

[20] Toombs, Jill. "Cakes By Jill". WordPress. October 10th, 2010.
<http://cakesbyjill.wordpress.com/>
[21] "Teeccino; America's Favorite Coffee Alternative". Teeccino. October 10th, 2010.
<http://www.teeccino.com/>

Sometimes for me, it's not the taste of coffee or the caffeine rush that I'm craving, but simply the comfort of a hot drink in the morning to start up my day positively. Especially on a cold winter day! How about variations on steamed milk? That is actually my newest favorite beverage. Drink it plain or add a little bit of vanilla to it. Nutmeg, cinnamon, honey, maple syrup, caramel or flavored syrups such as peppermint and amaretto can also spice it up and add fun to your morning!

DO NOT SPEAK WITH A BREATHY VOICE

I touched on that during the chapter on voice stereotypes. It damages your vocal cords by letting too much air through, which dries the vocal cords out and creates discomfort.

DO NOT WHISPER

Lots of people are mistaken thinking that whispering will save their voice in moments of crisis. If you have a sore throat or are experiencing any kind of vocal fatigue, whispering will dry out your vocal cords and make your pain worse because of the overwhelming amount of air passing between the vocal cords. It is better to speak softly rather than whisper. Apply what you've learned so far. Place your voice properly in the mask and use just a little pressure with your support. That's all!

If you can, stay home and rest. Don't speak for the whole day or until your troubles are over. Visit an ear, nose and throat specialist if your symptoms persist for more than two weeks. Many singers are known to protect their voice by observing a silence regiment. Céline Dion is one of them. She doesn't speak on days she has to perform, but she carries a little notebook and writes in it to communicate.

DO NOT TUCK YOUR BELLY IN

I mentioned this before but letting your belly out when you breathe needs to be reiterated. Failing to do so sends pressure upward; lifting your larynx instead of allowing it to tilt naturally into a neutral position, and it squeezes the vocal cords. It was very difficult for me to let go of this habit at first because I felt very self-conscious thinking that it made me look fat. Unless you wear clothes that are too tight for you, this should not be noticeable. Relax, breathe freely and—what the heck—let your belly out!

DO . . .

DO DRINK, DRINK AND DRINK WATER!

You must keep your body hydrated throughout your school day. Don't forget to gargle room temperature water to quickly lubricate your throat and your vocal cords if they suddenly feel dry. That happens to me sometimes when I'm nervous or if the room is very hot in September or June. Air-conditioned environments also trigger vocal dryness. And, of course, let's not forget that your vocal cords might feel dry if you haven't followed the "Don't" tips above!

Some will argue that drinking distilled or spring water instead of tap water is healthier for you and your voice. I would like to agree with that. However, since I tend to drink lots of it, it is simply impossible for me to carry so many bottles of water to school since I use public transportation to commute or ride my bike and recently my scooter to school. If you do choose to drink tap water at school, make sure to let the water run at least five minutes at cold temperature first thing in the morning to allow unwanted contaminants and residue that might have become stagnant in the pipes overnight, to clear. This particularly applies to old buildings that might have galvanized pipes, which are a source of lead in the water.

Most schools don't provide distilled or spring water for their staff but an idea would be to bring this up at your next staff meeting. If there is enough interest, the school or staff together might decide to subsidize distilled or spring water the same way it sometimes does for coffee.

If that isn't possible, equip yourself with a personal water filtration system. There are many brands available for different qualities and efficiencies. I bought the Brita[22] Faucet Filtration System and the pitcher and I was really impressed by the difference in the taste of the water with both. I would highly recommend them both as a fairly cheap investment. You can also buy a portable filtered water bottle like the one at waterbobble.com[23].

Drinking tap water is also considered "green"! In Canada, Jean Perrault, president of the Federation of Canadian Municipalities, urges municipalities to ban selling bottles of water in certain buildings because "bottling and shipping water consumes significant quantities of energy, and says that most water bottles end up in garbage dumps, even though they are recyclable."[24]

It makes sense financially to promote home water filtration as opposed to buying bottle water. I find the following argument quite convincing:

"If the cost ($100 or less) of purchasing a filter for your home causes you to hesitate, consider this: You can

---

[22] "Brita Products: Faucet Filtration", <u>Brita Water Filtration</u>. October 10th, 2010. <http://www.brita.ca/>
[23] "Bobble; Make Water Better", Bobble. October 10th, 2010. <http://www.waterbottle.com>
[24] Spears, John. "Going to Town on Bottle Water", <u>The Star</u>. March 8th, 2009. The Toronto Star. October 10th, 2010. <http://www.thestar.com/news/canada/article/598500#Comments>

buy a half-liter of bottled water for $1.35. If you filled this same bottle with filtered tap water once a day, it would take roughly 10 years before you spent that $1.35. However, if you purchased one bottle of water every day, after 10 years you will have spent $4,927.50."[25] This might be your opportunity to contribute and save both your money and the planet! So, drink, drink, drink and drink! Your body will thank you for it.

DO SPEAK AT LOW VOLUME

If your voice is placed in the mask and you are using your support properly when you address your class, there should be no need to increase the volume of your voice unnecessarily. It should project naturally without additional effort on your part. If your students still cannot hear you, they must quiet down for you to be heard rather than you raising your voice on top of theirs.

Set the expectation early on in September that when you talk, there should be absolutely no noise. Do not compromise on that. Get your class' attention at the end of a group activity by flicking the lights, clapping your hands or using a rain stick. These are old tricks that I'm sure you know but that we sometimes forget to use. Avoid using your voice to rally your class unless it is absolutely necessary.

Be self-aware of your speaking voice; make sure to listen to yourself when you talk. As soon as you notice yourself speaking too loudly, bring down your volume right away. Actually, when my class is working in teams, sometimes I notice when I speak that if I can hear myself over their noise, I'm being too loud and

[25] Meagan "Positively Green". "Get Off the Bottle and On the Filter", <u>Care 2 Make a Difference</u>. September 17th, 2009. Care2. October 10th, 2010.
<http://www.care2.com/greenliving/get-off-the-bottle-and-on-the-filter.html>

pushing my voice. Then, I speak more quietly with my normal volume and force myself to listen internally. I don't need to hear myself (because I already know what I'm saying) and they still hear me. Remember: never louder than lovely!

DO BREATHE THROUGH YOUR NOSE

Remember to breathe thought your nose as much as possible. It's very important because breathing through the nose filters and warms up the air before it goes down your pipes. Cold air quickly dries up your vocal cords and irritates your voice. Breathing through your nose also encourages deep breathing and helps focusing the voice in the mask by opening up your sinus cavities naturally.

DO EXERCISE TO KEEP YOUR BODY HEALTHY

Exercising may not be directly related to your voice but it has many overall benefits. When I was a kid, I used to practice synchronized swimming several hours a week. I took my sport very seriously, and I devoted up to twenty hours per week training at the community pool until I stopped around the age of fifteen. It helped me develop great lung capacity and physical endurance. I felt the positive effects on my health long into adulthood even though I had become much less active.

Sadly, everything changed when I hit my thirties! At that point, I felt that I didn't have as much energy as before to do everything that I wanted. I caught colds all the time and I felt depressed from being repeatedly sick. I also started teaching around that time, which made the matter worse because I was under a tremendous amount of stress to prove myself to my boss and colleagues and most importantly, students and parents! It's at that point that just as if I needed more problems, my ear, nose and throat specialist diagnosed tiny nodules starting to develop on my vocal cords.

What a wakeup call. I realized that I'd better start taking care of my body if I wanted to remedy my health problems and have a thriving teaching career. I dived back into researching vocal techniques. Totally by coincidence, I came across different articles debating the impact of exercising on physical and mental health. This might seem obvious to most people but it wasn't for me. In my mind, I associated sports with hobbies or weight loss. I thought I didn't have any extra time to spare towards another hobby, and secondly, since I have always been lucky enough to never have any weight problems, I just didn't consider exercising worth the time and effort.

But I decided to give it a try anyway. I bought a couple of five-pound dumbbells and made time every morning to exercise right before going to work. Free weights are rather inexpensive and can help you build a great resistance and strength program. (If you haven't exercised in a while, please consult a health professional for advice on creating a program that will best suit your needs.) Squats, sit-ups, push-ups and jogging are excellent inexpensive ways to exercise from home. I personally enjoy Pilates, swimming and jogging the best. Since I've started exercising I feel much better. Almost as soon as I started my new routine, my tendency to catch colds decreased, my energy level increased, and I was able to face the day more positively.

There are many reasons to explain that. The first reason is that exercising promotes the production of special chemicals, such as endorphins and epinephrine. They help your brain respond better to stress and make you more resilient. The American Psychology Association makes an interesting point in suggesting that "biologically, exercise seems to give the body a chance to practice dealing with stress. It forces the body's physiological systems - all of which are involved in the stress response - to communicate much more closely than usual."[26]   I thought that was particularly relevant.   Just think about the similarities between how your body reacts to exercising and stress: your temperature rises, you sweat, your heartbeat increases, et cetera.

The second reason is that exercising makes your immune system stronger.   Dr. Gabe Mirkin sums it up well in her article about how lack of exercising shortens lives.   She writes: *"When a germ gets into your body, you must make proteins called antibodies and cells to kill these germs.   However, antibodies and cells are made from protein, and the only place that you can store extra protein is in your muscles.   When you have large muscles, you can take the protein from muscles and make antibodies and cells.   When you have small muscles, you lack sources of amino acids to make proteins, and your immunity is inadequate to kill germs."*[27]

I found another benefit to exercising.   Not only do I get more energy from it, it also helps me relax.   When I can't sleep at night, I get up and exercise a little.   It allows me to release the stress of whatever is on my mind and it helps me going back to sleep.   Every time I've done that, I've been able to fall asleep minutes after exercising and going back to bed.

Since relaxation is key in successfully producing voice, always stretch before you exercise.   Go back to the beginning of the Daily Warm-up in Chapter Ten for some suggestions. Specific exercises can help you strengthen the muscles involved in supporting and projecting your voice.   Here are a few ideas to build up your abdomen:

---

[26] Dishman, Rod K. "Exercises Fuels The Brain's Stress Buffers", American Psychology Association. APA Help Center. October 10th, 2010.
<http://www.apa.org/helpcenter/exercise-stress.aspx>
[27] Mirkin, Dr. Gabe. "How Lack Of Exercises Shortens Lives", Dr Mirkin. January 12, 2001. DrMirkin.com. October 10, 2010. <http://www.drmirkin.com/fitness/9452.html>

Crunches, also referred to as curl-ups, are great to develop your abdominal muscles. Lie on your back, bend your knees, lift your feet at a 90-degree angle and pull your body off the floor. Your lower back  shouldn't leave the floor. There are many variations of crunches where you can bend your knees at various degrees or even keep your legs straight bringing them up and down as you pull your shoulders off the floor. You can also keep one leg straight at a 90-degree angle and the other about six inches to the ground and bring together elbows and knees alternatively. Repeat fifteen to twenty times for each repetition.

The Bridge: The Bridge consists of lifting your body off the floor as in the picture below. Hold this position for ten to twenty seconds or until you feel your muscles burning! I like this exercise because it allows me to really feel my back muscles in action. Be careful not to let your hips sink in; that would create unnecessary strain on your lower back. On the other hand, don't lift up your bum too much or you won't get the benefits of the exercise. Try to keep your back and legs as straight as an ironing board!

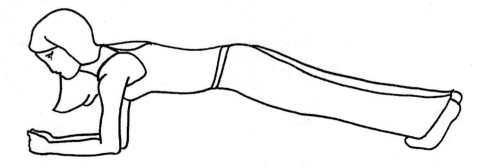

Squats: I have already explained how to do squats in an earlier chapter but question of refreshing your memory, here it is again! Start by standing up straight and pull your shoulders back with both hands above your hips. Place your feet shoulder length apart. Inhale and descend, keeping your knees in line with your feet. Keep your back straight and never look down. Descend until your tights have a 90-degree angle to the ground. Come back to a standing position without bouncing at the bottom. Exhale at the same time, focusing on your downward pressure as if you were propelling yourself off the ground. Keep your ribs expanded as long as you can. Repeat fifteen to twenty times.

I hope you can see the subtle relationship between exercising and your voice. A healthy body and mind give you more control over using your voice during the day: More control to place it in the mask, more endurance to control your support, and better resiliency to turn around any stressful situation to your advantage. Make time during your schedule to exercise. Get up one hour earlier everyday or go to the gym after school; make it work for you!

DO REST!
There is nothing worse than lack of sleep to lessen your chances at fighting germs and viruses, controlling your moods and your voice! Listen to what your body tells you when it aches all over. Use your time proficiently and get organized to accomplish as much as you can during the day. Don't wait until you are completely exhausted. Go to bed early and always get lots of sleep.

Seven to eight hours of sleep a night is the recommended time of sleep for adults. However, for some it's not enough to feel refreshed in the morning, and others would like to be able to spend less time sleeping and more time awake. I recently discovered that it is not how long one sleeps but the *amount* of sleep one gets that makes a difference in whether or not the body feels rested. Extensive research shows that the human sleep pattern is divided into five stages. Together, they form a cycle that takes approximately 90 minutes to complete. It repeats itself during sleep. To feel refreshed in the morning, you should sleep a number of hours equal to a multiple of 90 minutes. For example: four and a half hours, six hours, seven and a half hours, nine hours, et cetera.

Interestingly, it would be better than seven or eight hours of sleep simply because they are not multiples of 90 minutes. When a cycle is suddenly interrupted by your alarm clock, so is the brain activity releasing chemicals in your body and paralyzing your muscles during sleep allowing you to recuperate. Notice how many hours of sleep you get when you don't set up the alarm and wake up naturally to see if the result matches a 90-minute multiple.

Another productive way to maximize your energy is to sleep less (still keeping a multiple of 90 minutes) and combine your hours of sleep with another 90-minute nap in the evening. For example, four and a half hours of sleep added to a 90-minute nap would be more beneficial to you than sleeping a full eight hours. It seems that going into adulthood and having to follow the stiff expectations of a nine to five schedule, we have lost the concept of napping. Babies and animals set great examples for us to follow. Dividing your sleep pattern into several episodes is biologically natural and healthier.

DO KEEP YOUR CLASSROOM CLEAN

Even though caretakers in my school do an excellent job at sweeping the floors and everything else that their work encompasses, if I don't take it upon myself to wash the blackboards, dust off the shelves and make it a weekly class activity to wash the desks, the classroom becomes a true dust and germ lab. Airborne allergens, germs and vii enemies of the voice! More on that later...

DO STAY AWAY FROM MEDICATION WHEN POSSIBLE

I wouldn't recommend you to go against your doctor's advice so please use common sense with this suggestion! When possible for minor issues, try to find another alternative to medication because many of them have a negative effect on the voice. Don't forget to tell your doctor if you take herbal remedies since it can also interact with conventional medicine. You might find it useful to know which medication is better for the voice when it comes to side effects. The following website page from the Voice Academy has a comprehensive list of drugs and their impact on the voice: http://www.uiowa.edu/~shcvoice/rx.html.[28]

I have many natural alternative suggestions for you in the coming chapters, especially when it comes to dealing with allergies and the common cold. But there is one thing I would like to mention that particularly affects women and, knowing that women represent a greater proportion of the teaching field, this might be of special interest: PMS! The premenstrual syndrome does influence the voice indirectly with symptoms like tiredness, upset stomach, mood swings, difficulty concentrating, anxiety, et cetera.

There is an herbal product called Emerita Phytoestrogen[29] and supplements containing soy isoflavonoids that can help appease symptoms considerably by reestablishing hormonal balance. Remember, your body is your instrument; all that affects your body and soul can reflect onto your voice. Good luck! At this point, we are ready to look into how allergies and food sensitivities influence the voice.

---

[28] "Check Your Meds: Do They Affect Your Voice?", Voice Academy. October 10th, 2010. <http://www.uiowa.edu/~shcvoice/rx.html>
[29] "Emerita Products: PMS and Peri-Menopause", Emerita. October 10th, 2010. <http://www.emerita.com/index.cfm/category/4/perimenopause.cfm>

CHAPTER TWELVE
Fighting Allergies

If you've followed this book to the T so far and you are still having some vocal difficulty, it could be the result of allergies. Allergies are often problematic for the voice. If you suffer from allergies, your immune system has a tendency to overreact against antigens by producing histamine in your blood cells. This creates an inflammatory trigger effect in the surrounding tissue that can often be reflected directly in your voice or indirectly in your general physical state or state of mind. You might or might not be aware of all the things you are allergic or sensitive to as the response to allergens from your body may vary quite a bit and translate in different forms. If you have at least one known allergy or sensitivity, it doesn't matter if the antigens are airborne or food related. This hypersensitivity makes you predisposed to possibly many other kinds as well.

FEED YOUR VOICE AGAINST ALLERGIES

There is a very close correlation between allergies and food. I believe that you can use what you eat as a tool to fight allergies and preserve a healthy instrument. I have drawn many conclusions from my own personal experiences with food sensitivities and airborne allergies that I'd like to explain a little bit so you can understand how I came up with a theory that has helped me almost completely eliminate reactions to airborne allergens and food. It's a little long but I think I need to make a point so you can understand how it works!

I have spent probably the last ten years of my life trying to figure out how to get around allergies medication-free, simply because I don't like to take over-the-counter drugs. I started being allergic to grass and alder pollen as a kid. With only a little bit of a runny nose and congestion, my seasonal allergies didn't bother me too much then. I kept things under control by taking antihistamine medication during the month of July and I was fine, but my seasonal allergies worsened as I grew older.

When I hit my early twenties, I started having sensitivity reactions to food but I didn't know what it was at first. I started having hive episodes from time to time without warning. It covered my entire face and body and my skin itched for several hours. During a hive attack, what appeared to the casual eye as a hundred swollen mosquito bites on my face made strangers do a double take on the street and give me a second look. I'm not kidding! It was really ugly and embarrassing.

I once traveled to Chicago to see my favorite band and had a hive attack after eating Chicago's famous stuffed pizza. I was so embarrassed by the hive breakout that I hid in my hotel room for the next two hours until it went away, and while I saw the main act, I missed the opening bands of the night.

In addition, I struggled with minor skin problems until my early thirties, believing I was suffering from light acne. That particularly bothered me because it made me feel self-conscious to stand in front of my students whom I thought might judge me. It impacted my self-esteem and, consequently, my self-confidence since none of the over-the-counter and prescribed medications I tried resolved my skin issues. The hives kept coming back and I continued to feel insecure about my imperfect complexion.

TELL ME WHAT YOU EAT...
I'll Tell You Who You Are! I slowly started noticing a relationship between food and my skin issues especially when I was having hive attacks. My skin always broke out about half an

hour after my meals; it was no coincidence. I started keeping a journal of my eating habits to see if there was any type of food or particular ingredients triggering the reactions. I soon found citric acid, a common preservative agent in most packaged food, guilty as charged. When I stopped buying food with citric acid in it, my hives completely disappeared.

I still had a little bit of acne though which I later found out was really rosacea, a condition that easily makes one's skin flush, redden and break out. What I learned about rosacea is that it is, in some cases, a reaction to food sensitivity. It puzzled me because I had already eliminated food with preservatives or artificial ingredients from my diet. I once again kept a journal of my daily food intake versus my skin flare-ups since it was still getting itchy after meals (without the hives). Over time, I realized that coffee and chocolate (both of which I'm very fond of and had almost every day), tomato sauce, red wine and citrus made my skin the itchiest. When I'd go on vacation or when I'd be sick and deprived of my usual diet, my skin would completely clear. Then I'd go back to my food routine and the flare-ups would return.

My last food reaction was the least severe and the one I noticed last because it revealed itself in the subtlest way. At one point during my teaching career I started noticing always having a little bit of phlegm in my throat after eating lunch. It was annoying to feel the need to clear my throat during teaching time in the afternoon. It turned out to be light acid reflux. It is a combination of all my allergies and food sensitivities that made me look into what else, if I were already eating healthy could make me sick?

Did you know that some food is more likely to make you sick even if it's natural and fresh? To answer this question, let us start by understanding how the body reacts against allergens. When an allergic reaction occurs, the body produces histamine (a protein) that dilates blood vessels. Headaches, irregular heartbeats ensuing from low blood pressure, skin sensations such as itching, burning and flushing, acid increase, causing reflux or stomach pain, respiratory discomfort as in nose congestion, and sneezing and wheezing is the result of tissue inflammation in response to the histamine being released.[30] Many of these symptoms will have direct or indirect effects on your vocal cords notably acid reflux and, most importantly, whatever affects your respiratory tract and your psychological state.

Still trying to figure out why I was getting sick from healthy food, I finally found a common denominator in most of the food I was getting a reaction from: histamine! All of a sudden, everything made sense to me! As a protein, it naturally occurs in food, which I never knew. Cheeses, alcoholic beverages, vinegars, certain fruits, fish, chocolate, carbonated drinks and tea all contain high levels of histamine.[31] It is understood that someone with any kind of allergies is twice as susceptible to react to one or more triggers in different ways; whether they are airborne or food-related. That gave me a brilliant idea: Would keeping low levels of histamine in my blood minimize my allergic/sensitivity responses and strengthen my defense mechanisms? My hypothesis was that controlling my histamine level by choosing carefully what I eat would decrease my body's vulnerability to both airborne and food triggers.

For instance, before allergy season I concentrated on eating food with low levels of histamine to prepare my body against my seasonal peak. And it worked! I have been nearly 100% allergy-free for two years. My hives are gone, my rosacea is under control and the acid reflux is gone, too. When I cheat on my

---

[30] "Allergy Center: Histamine and Antihistamines", Alpha Online. Environmed Research Inc. October 10th, 2010. <http://www.alphanutrition.com/allergy/antihistamines.htm>

[31] "Useful Information: Histamine Restricted Diet", International Chronic Urticaria Society. October 10th, 2010. <http://www.chronichives.com/pages/lowhistamine.htm#foodsource>

diet I know right away: a little hive spot will appear on my arm or leg, or my scalp and cheeks will start itching. That reminds me to be careful and so I return to the food that is right for me.

Here is a detailed chart of food containing low and high levels of histamine. Focus on or avoid these to keep your immune system strong against allergies and food sensitivities.

HISTAMINE IN FOOD[32]

Food Groups	Low Histamine Food	High Histamine Food
Milk and dairy	Plain milk and ricotta cheese	All cheese and yogurt
		Buttermilk
Breads and cereals	Any made with pure unbleached grain or flour	Bleached flour
	All plain grains, oat, wheat, puffed rice, rye and plain pasta	All other
Vegetables	Most fresh or frozen vegetables	Eggplant, pumpkin, spinach and tomato
Fruits	Apple, banana, cantaloupe, figs, grapefruit, grapes, honeydew, kiwi, lemon, mango, pear, rhubarb and watermelon	Apricot, cherry, cranberry, currant, date, loganberry, nectarine, orange, papaya, peach, pineapple, prune, plum, raisins, raspberry and strawberry
Proteins	All pure, freshly cooked meat and poultry	All fish and shellfish
		All processed and left-over cooked meat
	Most plain legumes and pure peanut butter	Soy, red beans, eggs
Nuts and seeds	Most nuts and seeds	Cocoa
Fats and oils	Pure butter and vegetable oil	Margarine

---

[32] "Useful Information: Histamine Restricted Diet", International Chronic Urticaria Society. October 10th, 2010. <http://www.chronichives.com/pages/lowhistamine.htm#foodsource>

I don't want to tell you to stop eating food with high levels of histamine completely unless they give you long-term or great discomfort. My suggestion is rather to carefully prepare yourself for your allergy season by focusing on food that will keep your blood levels of histamine low or to avoid eating these right before class (perhaps for breakfast, snack and lunch, for instance). The idea is to give your immune system a break. Save yourself the effort of always being under attack and therefore minimize the inconvenience of continuously being exposed to histamine.

Another way to decrease the level of histamine in your blood is to eat food that will naturally weaken its production.   Here is a quick chart of what foods will help counterbalance the effects of histamine.

OFFSETTING HISTAMINE[33]

WHAT TO EAT	ACTIVE INGREDIENT	WHAT IT DOES
Bright red, orange and yellow fruits and dark green vegetables	Vitamin C and other antioxidants	It's a natural antihistamine and anti-inflammatory.
Oily fish, nuts, seeds and their oils	Essential fatty acids	They have anti-inflammatory properties.
Garlic and onions, blue-green algae, spirulina, chlorella and kelp	Quercetin	It's an anti-inflammatory that stabilizes the release of histamine and boosts the immune system.
Ginger	Gingerols	It slows histamine production.

[33] "Summertime Allergies", The Food Doctor. The Food Doctor Ltd. October 10th, 2010.
<http://www.thefooddoctor.com/Summertime-Allergies-Ahealth_fdw_hayfever/>

You will notice that some of the red, orange and yellow fruits you might be thinking of probably also appear in the "high histamine food" column of the Histamine Food chart. You may react differently to some foods so choose them carefully. You will also notice that I haven't mentioned much about nuts even though they are the culprit of some of the most fatal allergies. It's because niacin, not histamine, is the enemy in nuts.

Everybody is different and that's exactly why allergies and food sensitivities are so difficult to diagnose. It felt important to share my experience with you just to show how diverse the list of food capable of disturbing your system can be. Keeping a journal of your eating habits is important to locate your own food hypersensitivity, intolerance, or allergy. Use the following daily tracking system to verify if what you eat affects your voice.

Food Allergy Journal

Week of _____

Day of the Week	Breakfast	Lunch	Dinner	Snacks
Monday	I ate:	I ate:	I ate:	I ate:
	Comments:			
Tuesday	I ate:	I ate:	I ate:	I ate:
	Comments:			
Wednesday	I ate:	I ate:	I ate:	I ate:
	Comments:			

	I ate:	I ate:	I ate:
Thursday	Comments:		
Friday	I ate:	I ate:	I ate:
	Comments:		
Saturday	I ate:	I ate:	I ate:
	Comments:		
Sunday	I ate:	I ate:	I ate:
	Comments:		

If you think you might suffer from food sensitivities, pay careful attention to mucus production on your vocal cords, nasal congestion, how your whole respiratory tract feels, headaches, and digestion difficulties. Write down everything you eat in a day, take note of any discomforts after your meals, and watch for any recurring symptoms and the food that might have caused them in the comment section.

On a closing note: To this day, my skin is perfectly clear since I meticulously watch for and eat food with low histamine levels. My seasonal allergies have decreased to the point where I barely notice them. My vocal health is great, with no more daily runny nose and congestion and no more mucus on my vocal cords. In addition, I realized that I sleep better now since I can breathe better, which means I have more energy.

I put one-hundred percent faith in my low histamine food theory. It takes commitment and dedication to change your diet around but it is possible and worthwhile. It really seems to be working for me and it makes me very happy, so try it and let me know if it works for you!

More Tips on Allergies

ON EATING TOO MUCH

Besides gaining weight, eating too much may have other noticeable negative repercussions on the voice. First, the diaphragm can't expand properly to support the voice on a full stomach because it is located right underneath it. In other words, it's harder to breathe when full. Remember: breath is like gas for your engine. If the breath is off, everything else is off too!

Secondly, it might also create a tendency for your stomach to produce more acid then necessary to digest food, causing acid reflux. One of my readers and retired teacher Cindy Shore-Beauvais was kind enough to share her personal experience with me and gave me permission to tell you as part of this book:

> "I taught French Immersion and Core French for many years. I have had problems with nodules and a very hoarse voice. I also sing in a choir. I went to an ENT and to a speech therapist, eventually joining the group program at St. Michael's Hospital in Toronto. I learned that I probably had acid reflux and learned how to control it. I took medication for a while, which didn't work very well. Neither did all the voice exercises I tried. I must admit that I wasn't very faithful at doing them. Finally, when I was able to lose about 80 pounds (I was very overweight), my vocal problems went away. I still sometimes get reflux, but not often enough to bother me."

Also remember to try ½ a teaspoon of organic apple cider in a cup of juice or water before your meals to help prevent acid reflux and re-establish balance in your stomach.

SIMPLE DETOXIFICATIONS

A few times a year, it is beneficial to cleanse your body of toxins. That reinforces your immune system against allergens and virus. There are different ways to do it. I tried different regiments such as detox products from the natural food stores, to a diet of eating nothing else but Red Delicious apples for three days, to drinking a shot of wheatgrass juice daily. They all worked great and made me feel rejuvenated afterwards. Please visit your local natural food store for different detox programs and consult your doctor for any health risks.

SMOOTHIES

Vitamin C is a fantastic oxidizing agent to fortify your immune system against allergies. For high natural Vitamin C intakes, mix a bunch of fruits and vegetables in your blender with some water. Smoothies are very filling and an excellent breakfast or lunch substitute. For protein content, use spinach or hemp hearts. Here are some of my low histamine (except for the Spinach-Carrot-Banana-Apple smootie), high Vitamin C favorite smoothie recipes:

SMOOTHIE RECIPES

Banana-Mango-Apple	Mango-Apple-Banana-Ginger	Lettuce-Kiwi-Banana-Apple
1 cup of water	1 cup of water	1 cup of water
2 bananas	2 mangos	6 leaves of romaine lettuce
1 mango	1 Granny Smith apple	4 kiwis
2 Granny Smith apples	1 banana	2 bananas
	1 inch of ginger	1 Red Delicious apple
Pear-Apple-Banana	**Spinach-Carrot-Banana-Apple**	**Banana-Hemp Hearts**
1 cup of water	1 cup of water	1 cup of milk
4 pears	2 cups of spinach	3 bananas
1 Granny Smith apple	1 cup of chopped carrots	2 tablespoons of hemp hearts
1 Red Delicious apple	1 banana	
1 banana	1 McIntosh apple	

These recipes will give you two to three generous servings. I usually pour in an actual capsule of vitamin C to act as a preservative. I was careful not to include fruits with high histamine, but if you feel lucky, try adding some pineapple, strawberries, oranges or whatever your hunger calls for. Being creative is part of the fun! Blend the ingredients gradually; one at a time rather than all at once. Add water or milk if the texture appears too thick. Refrigerate and serve. Enjoy!

PLAN TIME WITH YOUR CLASS TO CLEAN

I wish I could tell you to keep your windows closed so that dust and pollens won't get in your classroom, but considering that most schools don't have air conditioning, that would be a pretty hard thing to do unless you don't mind suffocating in the heat! That is why it is so important to clean your classroom often to get rid of these as much as possible. I know I already mentioned that briefly in an earlier chapter but I'd like to revisit this topic a little bit more in depth. Cleaning your classroom often doesn't take too long and it can really make a difference in your own wellbeing and in your students' ability to concentrate and do well in class. It teaches students the pride of cleanliness and organization skills. If you look at it through this perspective than it really doesn't take any time away from teaching the curriculum.

I keep a set of 25 sponges in my classroom. My students and I clean every Friday afternoon. I take on the task of spraying each desk myself with a little bit of soap to avoid any silly behavior (make sure to check with your custodian or direction for school/children-friendly and approved products). Students are also required to organize their work neatly and put away old activity sheets and other unidentified objects found in their desks! We take about twenty minutes to clean and organize the desks, wipe chalk off blackboards and dust the classroom library and blinds. It's nice to come back the next Monday to an almost spotless classroom. Health Canada[34] has

---

[34] "Environmental and Workplace Health: Indoor Air Quality – Tools for School Action Kit for Canadian Schools", <u>Health Canada</u>. December 9th, 2007. Government of Canada. October 10th, 2010.

an action kit to help maintain indoor air quality in schools. Visit their website for more info!

PERSONAL AIR PURIFIER

Adding an air purifier system to your furnace is a great way to control the indoor quality of your home. Conventional air purifiers come in many sizes and can be installed directly on your furnace with or without filters (HEPA, Ionic, UV and Multi-Tech). I can say from personal experience that home air purifiers are generally quite efficient and I would certainly recommend them in your home if you suffer from airborne allergies or asthma.

For your actual classroom, small air purifier appliances are also available on the market anywhere between two to five hundred dollars. If you choose to go that route, make sure to check for the right square footage coverage to match the size of your classroom

Wouldn't it be cool if you could also have control over the air you breathe anywhere you go? Well, a couple of years ago, I came across a little gadget called the Mini-Mate that does just that. It is a personal air purifier no bigger than a cell phone (but much lighter) that you can wear around your neck. It is fabricated by Wein Products. Wein's Mini-Mate is a lightweight, filterless air purifier that uses electrical ions to destroy allergens and bacteria in the air. "Weighing in at a sleek 1.5 ounces, this air supply will help to purify your breathing space with the most powerful output available.[35]" The air coming out of the unit feels refreshing and pure.

I bought the Mini-Mate for my husband a while ago. He suffered from asthma and he was struggling in the subway on smoggy days here in Toronto. The Mini-Mate improved his

---

[35] "Air Supply Mini-Mate Wearable Air Purifier", Wein Products. 1997-2009 Wein Products Inc. October 10, 2010. <http://www.weinproducts.com/minimate.htm>

condition and he didn't need his asthma puffer when he wore it. I've also borrowed it to fly as I always find the air quality in airplanes to be rather poor, and the news a while back of a man infected with a strand of tuberculosis[36] flying to and from Europe despite his contagious condition wasn't reassuring. This illustrates perfectly the threat of allergens and the potential spread of viral infections in a confined environment: dusty classrooms with poor air circulation, no air conditioning and crowded with children come to mind immediately. It is difficult for the immune system to fight these potential hazards when we are interacting with so many infected carriers every day. No wonder our immune system can't keep up the battle.

The Mini-Mate can be a great ally. The only disappointment in the Mini-Mate is its price. It comes with a price tag of over $100.00, almost $200.00 with the purchase of rechargeable lithium ion batteries and a charger. Further positive testimonies and scientific credits back up the Mini-Mate on the Wein Products website at: www.weinproducts.com. Take a few minutes to visit it and judge for yourself.

SALT ROCK CRYSTAL LAMPS

Negative ions occur naturally in nature. They are in abundance in the air near waterfalls, mountains, beaches and forests. They are created by forces of rainstorms, cascading water, lightning, sunlight, ocean waves and wind. After an electric thunderstorm a powerful negative ion generator, for example, the air feels pure and refreshing. Absorbing negative ions in the air of such environments with our lungs and skin pores is energizing. When our blood cells contain high levels of negative ions, they

---

[36] "Nobody At Risk, TB Patient Says", Canada.com. July 12th, 2007. The Windsor Star and CanWest MediaWorks Publications Inc. October 10th, 2010. <http://www.canada.com/nationalpost/news/story.html?id=920327a3-838d-4e3c-b641-e2ced7366954>

are better suited to follow a healthy metabolic process and our body pH remains alkalized. Positive ions (free radicals), on the other hand, slow down the metabolism process, making us sick and depressed. That is explained because "negative ions neutralize pollutants and provide positive effects on health to:

- Stimulate the reticulo-endothelial system, a group of defense cells in our bodies that marshal our resistance to disease.

- Act on our capacity to absorb and utilize oxygen. Negative ions in the bloodstream accelerate the delivery of oxygen to our cells and tissues.

- Speed up oxidation of serotonin (5-hydroxtryptamine) in the blood. This is well-known to have far-reaching effects on mood, pain relief and sexual drive."[37]

Our time spent inside in sealed buildings surrounded by free radical-producing household machines (televisions, computers, ventilation systems, fluorescent lighting, et cetera) in highly polluted metropolitan city centers and away from the country deprives us from healthy doses of negative ions. To restore balance between negative and positive ions in my house, I got myself a couple of Salt Rock Crystal Lamps. They come from the Himalayan Mountains and the heat produced by the light bulb against the crystal salt generates negative ions. It cleans the air of pollutants, allergens, dust, bacteria and mold pores. I think it's fantastic! I've seen them sold in natural food stores, hardware stores, alternative medicine shops, and online.

They are not very common and yet not difficult to find if you make the effort of looking them up. They are sculpted in

---

[37] "Physiological Benefits of Negative Ions on the Human Body", <u>Oriental Detox.</u> October 10th, 2010. <<u>http://www.orientaldetox.com/negative-ions.html</u>>

different shapes for your liking. Each lamp is unique by its peach and white color variations. I find them very beautiful! When turned on, the soft peach light is calming and inviting. When I leave my lamps on for several hours, I do notice a difference: the air I breathe is revitalizing! I love my crystal lamps so much that I actually got my parents one each for Christmas!

ABOUT DOING LAUNDRY
Do not hang your laundry out to dry. Use a dryer instead during your seasonal peak to avoid breathing in pollens stuck on your clothes, and carrying them around all day long! I have also heard of a laundry additive that removes allergens but I haven't personally tried it. For better rest periods, clean bedding weekly in hot water using baking soda for whites instead of common laundry detergents that often contain harmful dyes, perfumes and other chemicals.

VASELINE
One beautiful June morning, I kept sneezing when I went to pick up my class after the first bell. One parent shared with me a tip on avoiding allergies: put a little bit of Vaseline in your nostrils to trap allergens. I tried it and it seems to work! I think keeping the inside lining of the nose from dehydrating thanks to the Vaseline also keeps the common cold and flu virus from adhering to the vulnerable nostril membranes. Great idea! It would probably be even healthier to use un-petroleum jelly. Try NasoGel[38] by NeilMed or use a bit of sesame oil. More on the common cold and flu viruses in the next chapter...

---

[38] "NasoGel Moisturizer For Dry Noses", NeilMed. 2000-2010 NeilMed Pharmaceutical Inc. October 10th, 2010. <http://www.neilmed.com/can/nasogel.php>

CHAPTER THIRTEEN
Fighting the Common Cold

As soon as winter comes, common cold viruses resurface in classrooms all around the globe. It doesn't matter if you live in a warm or cold environment; weather changes have nothing to do with catching colds. The same goes for a weak immune system. You might exercise, eat right, take food supplements and still catch colds. Common colds strike adults on average two to three times a year while the frequency of infection in children increases in average between six to ten times yearly. There are hundreds of different strands of the common cold virus, which makes it nearly impossible to eliminate. The common cold and influenza viruses have several similarities when it comes to symptoms; therefore, any of my advice on preventing and treating a cold can apply to the flu as well with varying degrees of effectiveness.

Being a teacher, I feel particularly vulnerable in the face of the common cold and flu. At some point, the daily exposure to sick kids in my classroom became overwhelming and my body just couldn't handle it anymore. During the 2005-2006 school years, it seemed that my helplessness to colds peaked; I caught seven colds between November and April those years. Enough is enough, I thought; this nonsense has to end!

Every time I'd catch a cold, I'd try something new that I might have read about on the Internet or heard of by word of mouth. I unsuccessfully tried numerous natural products, homeopathy, home remedies and over-the-counter medications. This was quite a frustrating process because none of the advice I received really seemed to prevent any of my symptoms or shorten their length. I always develop the same symptom pattern:

1) At the onset of a cold, I feel a slight irritation or dryness sensation behind my soft palate and my nose feels dry.

2) A few days later, I get a runny nose.

3) My nose gets congested.

4) I get the chills.

5) I develop a sore throat.

6) I start coughing.

HOME REMEDIES AND PREVENTIVE MEASURES
There are many known methods to help your body heal itself from the cold virus—or at least alleviate the symptoms. The value in home remedies is debatable as their effectiveness varies from one person to another. Here are a few non-medical solutions to colds that significantly (although not always completely) work for me. Please keep in mind that none of my suggestions are intended to diagnose, treat, cure or prevent colds. Consult your family doctor or a health specialist before using any of the following.

Vitamin C is a powerful antioxidant that helps produce white cells (responsible for destroying viruses and bacteria) in your blood while limiting the amount of histamine being released. Your immune system will benefit from it as soon as a cold is contracted. Because it is non-toxic, you can take at least 1000mg every hour for the first six hours. Then, decrease your dosage to six times daily[39] until you feel better. Long-term intake of vitamin C (1000mg daily) is a great supplement to a healthy diet and will increase your overall resistance to viruses.

Echinacea is an herb with some antibacterial and anti-inflammatory properties that may relieve your cold symptoms. I have not seen much improvement after using Echinacea but so many of my friends praise it that I couldn't leave it out. Try it to see for yourself.

Ginger also has antihistamine qualities. Brew five two-inch pieces of peeled ginger roots (finely thinned) in boiling water. Let the water cool down and remove ginger after 15 to 20 minutes. Drink as is, at room temperature or cold. Instant honeyed ginger drinks are also sold in most Chinese and natural grocery stores. Ginger tisane helps alleviate nasal congestion, sore throats and fever. It's mostly a nice, spicy, feel-good beverage that I've come to appreciate during cold winter days, especially coming back from my recess duties!

Garlic is a popular antibiotic thanks to its unique chemical component: allicin. It boosts the immune system by preserving levels of antioxidants. It is most effective in treating colds if taken prior to the symptoms showing or as soon as they appear. The recommended dosage is two to three raw garlic cloves or two to three 300mg tablets[40] daily. As much as it might do you good, it might as well do you harm if you have food sensitivities or intolerances. Do not take it excessively and be on alert for possible allergic reactions such as stomach disturbance, skin

---

[39] "Cold & flu and Vitamin C", C For Yourself. 1997-2008 Cforyourself. October 10th, 2010. <http://www.cforyourself.com/Conditions/Colds___Flu/colds___flu.html>
[40] "Diet & Nutrition: Garlic", Health 24. 2000-2010 October 10th, 2010. <http://www.health24.com/dietnfood/Healthy_foods/15-18-20-143.asp>

rashes or even asthma. Garlic might also interfere with certain medications, so please consult your doctor.

Chicken soup is the number one comfort food when you feel under the weather. It is probably the oldest home remedy of all, passed down from generation to generation. There are many theories to explain why it reduces cold symptoms so effectively. To start with, inhaling its steam helps in opening a stuffy nose's airways. Others argue that the soup's spice combination—sometimes including pepper and garlic—may play a similar role.

Dr. Rennard, a specialist in pulmonary medicine, offers another credible hypothesis regarding chicken soup and colds. His research shows that chicken soup stops neutrophil, a form of mucus, from accumulating during white cells' production. As a result, there is less tissue inflammation and cold symptoms become less apparent. He even went as far as testing different brand-name soups to see which ones were the most successful. "Here's the list of brand name soups Rennard used - in order of how effective they were in slowing the progress of colds and flu.

1. Knorr's Chicken Flavor Chicken Noodle

2. Campbell's Home Cookin' Chicken Vegetable

3. Campbell's Healthy Request Chicken Noodle

4. Lipton Cup-O-Soup, Chicken Noodle

5. Progresso Chicken Noodle

6. Grandma's Soup

7. Health Valley 100% Natural Chicken Broth

8. Healthy Choice Thick and Heart Country Vegetable

9. Progresso Hearty Vegetable and Pasta

10. Campbell's Vegetarian Vegetable

11. Campbell's Vegetable Soup with Beef Stock

12. Health Valley Fat Free Garden Noodle

13. Cup O' Noodles, Oriental Nissin

14. Campbell's Ramen Noodles, Chicken Flavor"[41]

I couldn't move on to my next tip without providing you with a homemade chicken soup recipe. Lots of tender loving care will go a long way in treating one's cold. Knowing that someone took the time to prepare a chicken soup from scratch just for you is simply a very comforting feeling. Next time you, a family member or another loved one gets sick, why not try the following recipe graciously provided by my mother-in-law Rina? It's delicious; enjoy!

Ingredients:
1 large carrot
1 onion
2 celery branches with leaves for more flavor
8 to 10 black peppercorns
1 tablespoon of chicken broth
6 or 7 skinless and boneless chicken thighs
10 to 12 cups of cold water
½ cup of white basmati rice

Preparation:
Put all ingredients in a large pot and pour in cold water. Bring water to a boil, then cover partially and simmer for approximately 1 hour. Remove from heat and cool slightly. Remove the chicken tights from the pot and cut

---

[41] Day, Chet. "Chicken Soup: Nature's Best Cold and Flu Remedy?", Chet Day's Health & Beyond. 1993-2010 How to Beat Colds and Flu with 37 Natural Remedies and Three Healing Meditations. October 10th, 2010. <http://chetday.com/coldfluremedy.htm>

them out in small pieces. Remove cooked vegetables as well. Puree most chicken (put a little bit aside for later) and vegetables in blender. Add a cup of broth if the mixture seems too thick and finish blending until smooth. Pour back blended chicken and vegetables into the broth. Add the small chicken pieces you had previously put aside as well. That will thicken the broth and give it a colorful flavorful texture. Put the pot back on the stove and reheat over medium to low heat. Add rice and taste for seasoning with salt. Let it cook for 20 minutes. Bon appétit!

A Fixer Elixir is a special solution that can help eliminate bacteria leading to a sore throat. It can be used as a preventive measure or for treatment. Gargle the following fixer elixir provided to me from my good friend and mentor Jaime Vendera.

Ingredients:
1 tablespoon of organic apple cider vinegar
1 cup of water
¼ teaspoon of organic sea salt
¼ teaspoon of cayenne pepper
5-10 drops of organic lemon juice

Preparation:
Mix warm water with salt, cayenne pepper and lemon juice.[42] Gargle the solution for a few seconds to relieve the pain caused by a sore throat.

Honey and lemon combined in hot water is a soothing and calming drink to overcome a sore throat and congested nose.

---

[42] Vendera, Jaime. Raise Your Voice: Second Edition. Vendera Publishing, 2007, p.168

Another alternative use for lemon is to breathe in its steam from a boiling cup of water. For better results, simply place a towel over your head. A teaspoon of honey can also be swallowed on its own to coat and lubricate an otherwise dried and sore throat.

I have certain reservations about taking too much honey when you're sick with a cold. Its downside is that because it is a form of sugar, it will contribute to acidifying your body. The good news is that raw honey is the least acidifying sweetener. I will tell you more about body acidity versus alkalinity soon and you will understand what I mean.

Flushing your nose and sinuses the smart way can be tricky. Never sniff the mucus back up. Put a finger on one of your nostrils and gently blow your nose. If your nose is badly congested, you might be tempted to buy an over-the-counter nasal decongestant. The problem with decongesting nose drops or sprays is that they are highly addictive to the point that it will make your congestion worsen in the long run. You're not supposed to use decongestants for more than three days in a row while a cold typically lasts seven days. How does that make sense? I once ignored the warnings on the bottle. I had to use the spray more and more frequently until it didn't clear my congestion at all anymore. I went to see my doctor and he advised my only solution was to wait it out. It was a very awful wait! I know better now.

To flush the mucus out, I use NeilMed Sinus Rinse Nasal Wash.[43] It comes with ready-to-use saline solution packages for easy convenience. The principle behind this irrigation device is similar to the Neti pot (an ancient Ayurvedic cleansing technique) that I also own. Health food stores and some drugstores sell those as well. Both are simple to use. Fill it up

---

[43] "Sinus Rinse TM Nasal Rinse", NeilMed. 2000-2010 NeilMed Pharmaceutical Inc. October 10th, 2010. <http://www.neilmed.com/can/sinusrinse.php>

with warm distilled or filtered water (never use tap water); add the saline solution or a teaspoon of table salt and half a teaspoon of baking soda to it. Place the bulging spout end of the NeilMed bottle or the Neti pot in one nostril and slightly tilt your head forward in the opposite direction to let the water come out by the other nostril.

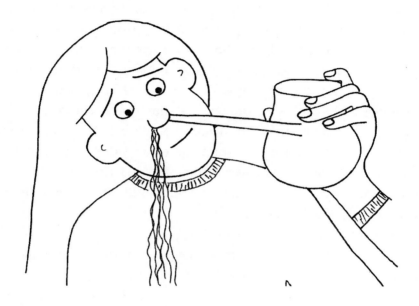

Letting a little bit of water flow gently in the back of your throat to lubricate and disinfect it is not a bad idea either. Incorporating a nasal rinse twice a day to your daily hygiene moistens the nasal mucous membrane and frees it from pollen, dust, chemicals or other pollutants. This is particularly recommended for people suffering from sinusitis, asthma and other pulmonary diseases.

Washing hands is effective against cold prevention. I have a vivid memory of my grade nine teacher demystifying the belief that colds are mostly spread through coughing and sneezing. I remember him very clearly explaining that when someone coughs or sneezes, it is not necessarily the droplets in the air that are the most likely to make their way to your airways, but rather the droplets on that person's hands transferred onto the doorknobs, computer keyboards, pencils, books, telephones, toys, et cetera, that you will pick up later.

He claimed that this had been tested with two groups of infected and healthy people. Scientists blended them and created two new groups. In one group, infected people were instructed to cough in the other's face for ten minutes. In the second group, participants shook hands for ten minutes. Surprisingly, more people got sick from shaking hands. Well, not exactly. It's not shaking hands that made them sick; it is carrying the virus from contaminated fingers to the nose or eyes afterwards. Children and adults have a tendency to put their hands to their face much too often. Even I do it all the time. Rubbing your eyes or nostrils is enough to introduce the virus to your body and start the infection.

My biology teacher advised that the cold virus could survive up to three hours on inanimate objects before someone else picks it up, but I have also read that it can last up to three days. I'm not sure which is accurate but beware. Classroom surfaces, doorknobs, grocery carts and hotel television remote controls are among the most likely objects to carry viruses so keep your hands off them!

The conclusion is: if you have a cold, cough or sneeze in your sleeve rather than covering your mouth with your hand; but most importantly, wash your hands often. That includes after blowing your nose as well to avoid spreading the virus in your environment. Sick or not, wash your hands often with warm water and soap and don't touch your face to avoid contracting or spreading the virus!

Calcium is a great asset in fighting colds. I discovered this recently after reading the book *Never Get Another Cold*[44] by Thomas Appell. I have been telling every interested teacher at my school about this book because it has helped me so much in my battle against colds. What you must know is that if your body has an acid alkaline imbalance—specifically a low pH (potential of hydrogen) level—this will create an environment for viruses and bacteria to grow. For that reason, the lower your pH level, the more acidic your body is and the higher your vulnerability is to colds, the flu and other illnesses as well. To reverse this process, you must decrease your acidity level by increasing your pH and make your body more alkaline. You can test your saliva or urine for your pH level using test strips.

pH RANGE CHART

Acid			Healthy Body pH Range				Alkaline			
<4.5	5.0	5.5	6.0	6.5	7.0	7.5	8.0	8.5	9.0	9.5+

Certain food is naturally prone to either acidify or alkalize your body. You will find on the next pages a complete alkaline to acidic food chart[45] for your easy reference.

---

44 Appell, Thomas. Never Get Another Cold. VDP Publishing, 2004.
45 "Food Charts: Alkaline/Acidic Food Charts", The Original Essense-Of-Life LLC. 2002-2010 Raw Food Composition and Nutrition Handbook. October 10th, 2010. <http://www.essense-of-life.com/moreinfo/foodcharts.htm>

Alkaline to Acidic Food

Rank	Vegetables	Fruits	Grains	Dairy	Pro-teins	Spices and Seasoning	Sweeteners	Miscellaneous	Drugs and Chemicals
Extremely Alkaline		-lemon -watermelon							
Alkaline Forming	-asparagus -vegetable juices	-cantaloupe -dates -figs -lime -mango -melons -papaya -grapes (sweet) -kiwi -passion fruit -pears -pineapple -raisins -fruit juices				-parsley			

Rank	Vegetables	Fruits	Grains	Dairy	Pro-teins	Spices and Season-ning	Sweete-ners	Miscel-laneous	Drugs and Chemi-cals
Moderately Alkaline	-beet -bell peppers -broccoli -lettuce -cabbage -cauliflower -alfalfa sprout -avocado -garlic -peas -potato -pumpkin -squash -sweet corn	-apple -grapes (sour) -orange -peach -apricot -banana (ripe) -currants -raspberry -strawber-ry -grapefruit -nectarine			-beans	-ginger -salt		-vinegar (apple cider)	
Slightly Alkaline	-artichoke -Brussels sprouts -cucumber -leeks -mushrooms -onion -pickles (homemade) -radish	-eggplant -olive -tomato			-soy beans -soy cheese -soy milk -tofu -sesame seeds			-mayonnaise -olive oil -yeast	

Rank	Vegetables	Fruits	Grains	Dairy	Proteins	Spices and Seasoning	Sweeteners	Miscellaneous	Drugs and Chemicals
Neutral		-blueberry		-butter (unsalted) -cream -cow milk -yogurt (plain)				-margarine -most oils	
Moderately Acidic	-popcorn (with salt And/or butter)	-cranberry -dry coconut -plum -prune	-barley -bran -cereals (unrefined) -crackers (unrefined rye, rice, wheat) oats (rye, organic) -pasta (whole grain) -rice (basmati and brown) -wheat bread	-butter (salted) -most cheeses -milk (homogenized)	-dried beans -egg white -most nuts -soy sauce -seeds (pumpkin, sunflower)		-fructose -honey (pasteurized) -maple syrup (unprocessed) -molasses (organic)	-ketchup -mustard	

Rank	Vegetables	Fruits	Grains	Dairy	Proteins	Spices and Seasoning	Sweeteners	Miscellaneous	Drugs and Chemicals
Extremely Acidic	-pickles (commercial)	-fruit juices with sugar -jams and jellies	-breads -cereals (refined) -flour (white wheat) -pasta (white) -pastries and cakes from white flour -whole wheat food	-yogurt (sweetened)	-beef -fish -lamb -pork -poultry -seafood	-table salt -(refined and ionized)	-artificial sweeteners -brown sugar -maple syrup (processed) -molasses (sulphured) -sugar (white)	-beer -carbonated soft drinks -chocolate -tea (black) -white vinegar -(processed) -wines -coffee -liquors	-cigarette and tobacco -drugs

Think about it: the cold and flu season starting in late fall and early winter is no coincidence. That corresponds perfectly with Halloween and the holidays. Why? Because we stuff ourselves with the biggest acidifying foods during that time window: sweets and alcohol. Another highly acidifying and popular food includes coffee. How many cups of coffee do you drink a day?

An indicator that coffee is unhealthy and addicting is that if you skip it one morning, your body will let you know with a sharp headache. It took my system about two weeks to completely rid itself from caffeine and get used to not having coffee in the morning. The headaches were a pain and I miss my delicious double espresso latte but it was all worthwhile in the end.

What about meat? The meat industry is extremely pollutant and the number one party responsible for global climate change. I think both our bodies and the environment would thank us if we could only decrease how much meat we eat. White breads and pasta are also extremely acidifying. I find it pretty hard not to have either one of them for a full day. Typically, I would have toast in the morning, a sandwich for lunch, and pasta two or three times a week for dinner. Now, I still have bread for breakfast, but I substitute the sandwich for raw veggies and fruits for lunch, and I try to eat pasta only once in a while.

One last observation: Did you notice that almost all fruits are alkaline? Lemon is actually the most alkaline of all citrus fruits. There is a false belief that citrus are acidic. In reality, the fruits themselves have an acid pH but they leave an alkaline residue in the body after being metabolized. Doesn't it all make sense to you now? So of course, cutting on sweets, alcohol and coffee will help balance your pH tremendously. Suggesting eliminating all acidifying foods would be ridiculous. In addition, that would bring your pH to the extreme other end of the spectrum, which would be as harmful. Too much is like not enough. Just be careful to balance your diet and eat plenty of fresh raw fruits and vegetables during the cold season or while you're sick.

One way to bring your pH level to the healthy body range is to take calcium tablets. It is easier for your body to assimilate calcium when it is taken with magnesium. Make sure to buy a quality product from a natural health food store rather than a generic brand name from your local drugstore. It's more expensive but it can make a huge difference! The daily recommended adult daily allowance is one to three tablets of 300mg of calcium and 150mg of magnesium. I usually take a couple more whenever I start feeling a cold coming.

SOME WINNING FOOD!
I was interested to see what food made it in both the alkalizing and low histamine (from the previous chapter's Histamine in Food chart) categories. You will see from this chart that vegetables are the big winners here, just like your momma always said: "Eat your vegetables!"

ALKALIZING AND LOW HISTAMINE FOOD

FOOD GROUPS	WINNING FOOD
Vegetables	Asparagus, beet, bell peppers, broccoli, lettuce, cabbage, cauliflower, alfalfa sprout, avocado, garlic, peas, potato, squash, sweet corn, artichoke, Brussels sprout, cucumber, leeks, mushroom, onion, pickles (homemade), radish.
Fruits	Lemon, watermelon, cantaloupe, grapes, mango, pear, apple, banana, grapefruit.
Milk and Dairy	Goat and cow milks, pure butter (unsalted).
Cereals	Barley, bran, cereals (unrefined), crackers (unrefined rye, rice, wheat), oats (rye, organic), pasta (whole grain), rice (basmati and brown), wheat bread.
Proteins	Beans, almond, chestnut, sesame seeds.
Spices and Seasonings	Parsley, ginger, sea salt.
Sweeteners	Honey (raw).

Again, keep in mind that a balanced diet is a must. Having a diversified menu with elements from all food groups is ideal. Only during specific times and for short periods should you cut back on certain food. At the end of the day, using your common sense is a must.

AN ALTERNATIVE TO LOZENGES

I've had moderate success with most of the home remedies and food diet I have just described. I want to tell you about a special oil that I discovered unexpectedly a few years ago. It's helped me attenuate cold and flu symptoms considerably to the point of annihilating them in as little as 72 hours. It was a real breakthrough for me because before I started using that oil, the nose stuffiness and coughing usually dragged for about three weeks. Then as soon as I'd start feeling good again, I'd get infected with yet another cold and the cycle began once more.

Before telling you my discovery, I must tell you how it came about. If you have ever set foot in Old Montreal during the mid-nineties, you might have heard my coloratura voice resonate throughout Place Jacques-Cartier where I was once regularly performing opera arias as a street artist. One day after my performance, a stranger introduced himself to me, mentioning that he was a professional opera singer and that he had even performed with the prestigious Metropolitan Opera in New York. It is needless to say that I was quite flattered that he took the time to come and talk to me. We chatted for a while, and before he left, he gave me a tiny bottle of essential oils. The label was so old that I couldn't see exactly what it was. But it didn't matter; I trusted him. He insisted that I should take a couple drops of it on my tongue whenever I felt voice fatigue. He said that it would soothe my throat and surprisingly, it did. I followed his advice religiously until my bottle ran out. I tried to get myself another bottle of this mysterious essential oil to no avail. I tried several natural health food stores in my area but the distinctive tiny bottle was impossible to find.

I never gave up on my quest. Whenever I had a chance to go to new health food stores, I'd check if it were sold there. One day, I was speaking to my mom on the phone. I had a very bad cough that I had been carrying all winter from repeatedly getting sick. My mom told me about an essential oil her naturopath had given her to treat her coughing. She smoked at the time and she had developed a bad cough during Montreal's cold wintertime over the last few years. She mailed it to me the next day. I was in luck! I cannot tell you how amazed I was when I opened the parcel and recognized the same tiny bottle I had so relentlessly been looking for! About five years had already gone by before I finally got my hand on another bottle. I could clearly read the name on the label this time: Sun Breeze by Sunrider.[46] I looked it up on the internet and ordered enough bottles to last me a very long time. What a relief!

To overturn the common cold and flu symptoms in a few days with barely any nasal congestion and runny nose, but most importantly no sore throat, no coughing and no damage to my vocal cords, I use Sun Breeze as an alternative to lozenges. Remember: my recommendations are solely based on my personal experience and I would please remind you to consult your family doctor before embarking on any treatment.

Before I tell you more about how I use Sun Breeze, let us understand how the cold virus works. While researching this matter, I came across a very informative website www.commoncold.org. It explains that, "the nose contains shelf-like structures called turbinates, which help trap particles entering the nasal passages. Material deposited in the nose is transported by ciliary action to the back of the throat in 10-15 minutes. Cold viruses are believed to be carried to the back of the throat where they are deposited in the area of the adenoid. The adenoid is a lymph gland structure that contains cells to which cold viruses attach."[47]

This is exactly the area where I first feel the sensation of dryness or the slight irritation I was describing earlier. I'm sure that if you pay careful attention to what your body tells you, you will notice it as well the next time you contract the cold virus. The treatment is simple and shouldn't last more than a couple days.

---

[46] "Sunrider: Welcome to Sunrider International", SunRider. 2010 The Sunrider Corporation dba Sunrider International. October 10th, 2010. <www.sunrider.com>
[47] "Understanding the Common Cold: The Nose – Side View", Common Cold. 1999-2007 Commoncold Inc. October 10th, 2010. <http://www.commoncold.org/undrstnd.htm>

1) As soon as you feel this familiar sensation of dryness or a slight irritation in the upper back of your throat, behind your soft palate, put a couple drops of Sun Breeze on your tongue.

2) Repeat five to six times a day until your symptoms disappear.

3) Increase your calcium intake by a couple tablets a day for the duration of your symptoms.

4) Refrain from eating sweets, coffee and other highly acidifying and high histamine food until your symptoms are completely gone.

Sun Breeze works because once the virus is introduced inside the body through the nose by contaminated fingers, it starts multiplying rapidly. To defend itself against viral infections, the immune system uses inflammatory mediators such as histamine to protect the body. This activates pain nerve fibers and consequently, cold symptoms such as nasal congestion, runny nose, sore throat, coughing and fever ensue. Sun Breeze is a perfect mixture of menthol, cassia oil, mint extract, eucalyptus oil and camphor. All these herbs have anti-inflammatory powers.

According to Commoncold.org, "it takes 8-12 hours for the viral reproductive cycle to be completed and for new cold virus to be released in nasal secretions." The first cold symptoms appear towards the end of this incubation period. I'm convinced that using Sun Breeze oil as an anti-inflammatory as soon as the first symptoms appear neutralizes mediators responsible for them. And voilà! In two to three days, say goodbye to all your cold troubles! About 25% of people infected with the cold virus become well without developing symptoms and now you can, too.

Does menthol dry out the vocal cords? Probably. One has to weigh the pros and cons of catching a cold versus the vocal cords feeling slightly dry. I say if you have any concerns about getting dehydrated, just drink more water! I also always warn people to use Sun Breeze moderately and with common sense. It is very spicy and has a numbing effect on the throat and it is not advisable to use it before you're going to teach, use your voice extensively or prior to singing. If you do, be extremely aware of how you use your voice as not to force it. Overusing your voice would defeat the purpose of protecting your vocal cords against irritation.

Combining calcium intake, a low histamine diet and Sun Breeze has been by far one of the most successful preventive measures and home remedies for me. I have not been sick ever since I have been using those methods. I would lie if I said that I never get colds anymore. I still do, but because symptoms go away quickly and are minimal, I am not bothered so much anymore. No more congestion and barely any runny nose, no more fever, no more sore throat, no more coughing. To me, that is as good as it gets. But just when I thought my cold and flu control methods couldn't get any better, I discovered an even more efficient way to keep the virus away. Can you believe it?

OIL OF OREGANO

I heard from a professional musician friend that Oil of Oregano has many therapeutic uses and can knock off all kinds of infections and fight yeast and fungi. He attributed his health success to the powers of the oil so I started taking it too. I have to warn you: it tastes really nasty! Also, even though it is considered safe to use for most people, consult with a medical professional prior to doing so. Put two to three drops of Oil of Oregano under your tongue, morning and night. Let it sit without swallowing for as long as you can to avoid the bad taste and it will just absorb itself into your blood vessels. The good news is that my friend was right. What a miracle oil! I have not been sick at all since I've been using it.

The closest call I've had was on New Years Eve when my girlfriend and I decided to go out celebrate. She was quite sick, suffering from a cold, but I twisted her arm to come with me anyway since New Years Eve only comes once a year and I didn't want either of us to stay home feeling miserable! We had a fun night but when I got home, I started sensing a little bit of dryness in my throat. I combined the use of Sun Breeze and the Oil of Oregano for the next 24 hours every time the dryness came back, determined not to let the cold ruin the rest of my holiday! That was it. One day later, the dryness was completely gone and I haven't gotten sick since. Another bonus: Three days after I started using the oil daily, my skin became soft and smooth like it has never been before. I am thrilled!

DISCIPLINE AND MOTIVATION

Self-awareness is needed to catch the cold and flu symptoms as soon as they appear. Discipline and motivation are important in order to commit to a program that will help you fight the fight against viruses. Most importantly, consistency is crucial. Prepare your body ahead of time to fight the cold season. Taking calcium once in a while simply won't work. Drinking three cups of coffee everyday won't work either. If you truly want to spend a cold and flu-free winter, you must take proper action. Listen to what your body is telling you when fatigue takes over and your throat starts aching. Trust your intuition and annihilate the virus as soon as possible! Today, I feel healthy, strong, confident, ready to teach and happy. I feel ready to meet my students' needs and take up new life challenges.

Well, I feel I've prepared you to handle any cold situations. Now, let's discuss vocal loss and what you can do about it...

CHAPTER FOURTEEN
Voice Loss

If you're like me, you like talking a lot. I want my classroom to have an interactive lively setting, so I utilize a lot of call and respond strategies and I use my voice pretty much non-stop. There are times when myself and the kids "shut-up" to work quietly and focus but otherwise, oral communication plays a major role in my teaching style and reciprocally, in the kids' learning styles as well. Don't forget that on average, teachers do nearly two hours of voicing for eight hours of work[48] daily. In such circumstances, losing your voice can be quite dramatic. I come to your rescue with more of my favorite tips to help you prevent voice loss and recover quickly!

REST

Many of us show up to work when we're sick! Please don't spread your germs and take a sick day instead. If you lost your voice from an infection or voice misuse, your vocal cords need serious attention. More importantly, what they need the most is rest! Try not to speak for a full day to give your vocal cords a chance to recuperate. When your voice is gone, here is my friendly advice: for your own sake and everybody else's, stay home and shut up!

CHATTERVOX

If you experience voice loss repeatedly and attempts at placing your voice in the mask and supporting it have been

---

[48] Hunter, Eric J. "153rd ASA Meeting, Salt Lake City, UT. -How Much Do Teachers Talk? Do They Ever Get a Break?" Acoustical Society of America. October 10th, 2010. <http://www.acoustics.org/press/153rd/hunter.html>

unsuccessful, you might want to consider buying a portable voice amplifier. A reliable brand is called ChatterVox.[49] Most personal amplifiers come with a headset microphone or a small mic that you place close to your mouth. The amplifier is worn on your belt or the sound can be directed to bigger speakers for large spaces. Some school boards might even buy it for you if you support your request with an Ear, Nose and Throat doctor's recommendation.

I think a personal amplifier is a little bit of a bandaid solution. Ideally, it should only be used for a big classroom like a small auditorium. It should only be a last resort. I really want to see you resolve your voice problems at the root rather than camouflage it but that takes time. Therefore, a personal amplifier can provide support and relief during such transition periods. With that in mind, I stand by it 100 percent.

BE PROACTIVE

You must take the suggestions in this book to heart and apply them to make things happen. You cannot try things here and there sporadically and expect them to work. Maintaining your voice, preventing allergies and avoiding catching the common cold or the flu virus take dedication and drive. Choose a few ideas that you feel would be beneficial to you and commit to them 100%. There is no room for laziness and inconsistency. Plan time to warm-up your voice before class, exercise daily, stop smoking, eat healthier for the voice; whatever it is I really don't care as long as you DO IT and stick with it! Setting up goals and achieving them is rewarding and increases self-esteem. As your voice improves, you will want to keep going and add on to changing your lifestyle. If you do become ill or your voice isn't progressing as fast as you would want it to, don't give

---

[49] "ChatterVox : The Finest Portable Voice Amplifier", <u>Chatter Vox</u>. 2009 Asyst Communications Co. October 10th, 2010. <http://www.chattervox.com/desc.htm>

up. Give yourself some time and realize that your body needs some time to realign itself with your new way of life.

GET HELP!

Working with the voice is not easy. If you feel helpless on your own, don't hesitate to get help. Pair up with a friend or another teacher to give each other feedback and encouragement on how you're doing. Warming up the voice in the morning and practicing together can be fun! Plus, a second opinion always helps. Most importantly, visit your Ear, Nose and Throat specialist, communicate with a local vocal coach or send me an e-mail at voiceyourselfintheclassroom@gmail.com for advice. I will be happy to assist you the best I can on your voice journey. I am also available for private voice lessons. I can surely help you with your speaking or singing voice.

Technology has proven to eliminate borders. Online teaching is the future! It doesn't matter where you are in the world; I can be of assistance. I teach online with my webcam and Skype. With these tools, your online voice lesson will be as efficient as in person. By hearing the student's voice and seeing the person live, I can find specific strategies to improve one's tone placement and more. You can also visit my website to read my newsletters for additional voice information. All these resources are available to you so please don't hesitate to take advantage of them. If you're unsure as to how to do the exercises described in this book or simply need reassurance that you are on the right track, please give me a shout!

PART FOUR

My Classroom

CHAPTER FIFTEEN
The Silence Diet

Noise in the classroom is harmful to your voice as you might try to speak louder to be heard unconsciously or not, exhausting your natural strength. Noise also hinders your students' ability to hear what you say. Research shows that young learners and students with learning or hearing disabilities as well as those learning a second language are particularly vulnerable to noise. First grade students miss one in every six words spoken by their teachers on average.[50] As they get older, the skill to mentally bridge gaps for words that might have been missed is developed, but until then, the negatives can have a sneaky influence on one's academic success. From poor attention span to inactive participation to inadequately assimilating knowledge, the potential risks are scary and can have repercussions in many learning spheres.

Every single sound produced in your classroom reverberates on walls, furniture and floors. Basically, it will bounce off any hard surfaces and echo until it completely dissipates. When a sound takes longer than four seconds to dissipate, it contributes to a muddy-sounding environment. In poor acoustic conditions, the combination of the slightest murmurs, drumming fingers and tapping pencils on desks, erasers falling on the floor, snipping scissors, rocking chairs, roaring moving desks, people walking in the halls, ventilation, heating and cooling systems and noise from adjacent classrooms all create a potentially odious cacophony. Your voice totally looses itself in this dance

---

[50] "Loud Classroom Hurting Students: Audiologists", CTV. October 1, 2007 CTV Globe Media. October 10th, 2010.
<http://www.ctv.ca/servlet/ArticleNews/story/CTVNews/20071001/noisy_classrooms_07100 1/20071001?hub=Canada>

of sounds seemingly having a party of their own. What you say becomes unintelligible to most students sitting in the classroom. In such circumstances, it is not surprising that students have difficulty understanding words that come out of your mouth and worse, have an even harder time concentrating while you teach or during working time.

Decibel levels decidedly alter positively or negatively everyone's wellbeing. Classroom noise is often measured around 70 dB to 85 dB. Paradoxically, the expectation for ideal working conditions is that noise levels should be kept under 30 dB. Most teachers need to speak at least at a loudness level of 65 dB to be heard over the class. But what does a volume of 30 dB represent? Typically, it sounds like a quiet whisper heard from three feet away or the sound of rustling leaves. In comparison, a quiet street has an intensity level of 50 dB. A normal conversation is about 60 dB. The inside of a car reaches 70 dB. A food blender measures 90 dB and the inside of a subway equals 94 dB.[51] So 30 dB is quite quiet. But quiet is good. Quiet is calm and peaceful. Quiet is what we need!

One way to minimize sound reverberation to insulate your classroom is to favor sound-absorbing materials. Carpets would be great in theory but we all know how impractical they are in the classroom: they collect dust, allergens and undesired smells and just become plain nasty over the years. Instead, it is better to protect uncarpeted floors using tennis balls on chair legs. They are wonderful but somewhat expensive if purchased ready to use for that purpose. An option is to ask a tennis club in your community for donations or to collect tennis balls that end up on the roof of your school. Felt pads from your local hardware store are also pretty cool even though they are not as durable. Other solutions such as draperies instead of blinds to cover windows make a difference in reducing noise. Adding more cork

---

[51] "Decibel (dB): Acoustic/Noise", Handbook For Acoustic Ecology. 1978 World Soundscape Project, Simon Fraser University, and ARC Publications. October 10th, 2010. <http://www.sfu.ca/sonic-studio/handbook/Decibel.html>

bulletin boards in your classroom can also naturally prevent disruptive noise. But these are things on which you might not have control upon, especially if your school is run on a particularly tight budget.

Your goal should be to have a nearly silent classroom when you teach and while students work. To achieve that, you must follow what I call The Silence Diet. Here are the rules:

RULE #1: WHEN I TALK NOBODY TALKS!

Demand absolute silence when you address the class! You should not have to raise the intensity of your voice to be heard in a noisy environment. You will need one hundred percent cooperation from your students to achieve that, which is easier said than done! First, students must explicitly be made aware of how noise affects your ability to teach and their ability to learn. I often tell my students that every single one of them has the right to learn and nobody has the right to take that away. If someone disturbs the classroom by being noisy, it is understood that he or she is infringing on that very right and that is simply unacceptable.

The ability to remain quiet requires each student not to talk, not to play with any of the items in his or her desk (whatever they may be!) and not to move his or her hands, feet and body unnecessarily. It sounds like a lot, but kids can do it if they are trained to do it. Just like anything else one learns at school, it is a skill to be developed.

Sometimes I feel that it might sound a little controlling to expect students to stay still while someone talks and it does require everybody to conform but it is absolutely necessary and well worth the effort. After all, you define what is best for you and the students. I'm sure you've heard this: "Who's the boss of the classroom? The teacher. Who's the boss of your body? You." Sound familiar? You set the rules and it's up to the students to follow them. If they choose not to, they should be accountable and accept consequences.

When I began teaching, I was very flexible and a bit oblivious to classroom rules. I didn't care about how students sit and I thought that it was normal to let them talk to each other during work or even talk back to me as a form of freedom of expression. I thought that I could trust them to use their common sense to know when their words were appropriate or not. But frankly, it just didn't work! It came to a point where I started to feel bullied by my students and parents. It was brutal! It affected my self-esteem and my teaching confidence took a serious hit.

I learned that in general, some students always behave because it's the right thing to do but many need more direction and structure. Unfortunately, that's just the way it is. I experimented with different strategies to establish a quiet working environment. One afternoon in June, my grade seven students kept acting silly in my class. I told them I'd bring the class outside to play if they could take the following challenge: sit up straight and quietly for ten minutes. So I set my timer for ten minutes. Some students just didn't get it and kept making funny noises on purpose or tried talking to their neighbor, disrespecting the rule. I paused my timer every time and waited for everybody to be ready again before continuing. What really puzzled me is how many students lacked the will and self-control to still their body and remain quiet and were being disrespectful even with the promise of such a reward. It took about twenty minutes before my timer reached zero.

A year later, I moved to another school and started teaching grade one students for the first time. Going from seventh to first grade was quite an adjustment in itself and I had no clue about how to approach discipline with younger kids. Towards the end of October, I was completely unable to teach my class because of constant interruptions. That made everybody very frustrated and my voice particularly weak. That also coincided with when I started developing nodules on my vocal cords.

I went to my vice-principal for advice. She gave me what became the best advice in my young teaching career: "Stop teaching for a while to re-establish rules and routines in your classroom." At first, I thought not teaching my class would be a little odd but then I understood what she meant: There is no point in teaching students that aren't ready to learn. It made a lot of sense but I was scared of how long it might be before I could start teaching the curriculum again. She assured me that I should take as long as I needed.

What exactly was I supposed to teach if I wasn't teaching languages, mathematics, or sciences? Then it hit me. I remembered that June afternoon with my seventh grade students. I ought to teach kids self-control and focus in order to remain quiet. I called this concentration skill "being respectful". Kids generally have a vague idea of what being respectful means but they don't actually know how to apply that notion in a classroom situation because nobody really takes the time to teach them how. We assume that this is an acquired self-explanatory skill (especially as kids get older) but it's not. So this is the strategy that I started using with my class from that moment on and that I'm still using today. Starting the first day of September, I teach the kids to sit properly at the carpet, interlacing their hands and crossing their legs. They have to remain quiet and more or less still for one minute. I set my timer as described earlier and pause it when someone breaks the rule by talking or moving during the next minute. When the timer reaches zero, we celebrate with a silent clap, hands in the air or a pad on the back. It's fun and relaxing! A detailed lesson plan is available at the end of this book for your easy reference.

RULE #2: PRACTICE, PRACTICE, AND PRACTICE!
The key for the Silence Diet to work is to practice often. Practice being respectful as much as possible in the beginning. When I first tried the Silent Diet with my energetic first grade students, they had such a hard time that being respectful was practically all we did for a few days. We practiced being respectful at the carpet. Then we practiced at the desks. Then, we did a tiny bit

of regular work and we practiced being respectful at the desks again. Coming back from recess, we practiced walking in a straight line in the hall quietly for a little while. We practiced repeatedly until we were able to stay quiet and still for one minute without pausing the timer before it reached zero. Eventually, students got so bored of practicing being respectful that they just wanted to get it over with as quickly as possible so they could actually learn and get some "fun" work done!

When I teach, everybody has to be respectful (that is sitting properly and being quiet) or I stop everything. I wait until everybody is ready before I continue. The same applies during a student presentation. The presenter will wait and demand that his or her classmates show that learning readiness before starting. If it takes too long, I get my timer out and we practice being respectful again! Once in a while during class, I say, "Okay guys, let's be respectful now!" and every student instantly gets into position. I don't necessarily use my timer then but I use "Let's be respectful please!" like a catch phrase to get everybody's attention. Give it a little bit of rhythm and melody and it can become a powerful call and response phrase. When I teach at the carpet and someone forgets to be respectful, all I have to do is put my hands together and look at the kid in question while I continue talking and he or she reverts back to position. When we go to a school assembly, I use the same body language and my students are all respectful and quiet. After a while, this becomes second nature to students and other rotary teachers often positively comment to me on the way my class sits quietly for them as well. It's wonderful!

RULE #3: RIGID CLASSROOM MANAGEMENT IS A MUST!
A former colleague of mine used to say "Hands are trouble; put them in prison!" Kids get a kick out of this funny way to illustrate how interlacing hands helps to keep them under control and stay focused. It is necessary to have an efficient discipline program in place that will allow you to reprimand

students that refuse to follow the Silence Diet of being respectful or who lack self-control and will, while rewarding others.

Some kids always follow the rules because they are eager to please. That's fantastic! For everybody else, we must teach the behaviors we want to see while they are under our supervision. There is a multitude of winning strategies out there. Two components make a strategy effective: First, students should be able to easily know how to do what's expected of them. Second, the rewards and consequences must be meaningful to them.

My favorite strategy is The Road Light System. You have probably heard of it before. This is how it works: I use a calendar and weather pocket chart measuring approximately 78cm x 112cm (30¾" x 44¼"). I don't actually need the weather, dates, days of the week and month cards but since I need the same number of storage pockets as I have students in my classroom, this particular style is perfect for The Road Light System. I identify each pocket with the names of my students using a dry-erase or washable marker. I create as many green, yellow and red construction paper cards, (small enough to fit in the pockets) as there are students in my classroom. I fill each pocket with a set of green, yellow and red cards, and hang my pocket chart where it will be noticeable in the classroom— preferably at the front. It must also be of easy access to me.

Let's step back and talk about how to use The Road Light System and specifically what the colors signify. It's quite simple. Everybody starts the day with a green card. The green cards mean that one is going through his/her day wonderfully with no obstacles on his/her path. After having reminded a student to follow the classroom rules a few times, I change his/her card to yellow: it's time to slow down and reflect on what the rules are and apply them better. If teacher promptings continue and that student refuses to cooperate, I change his/her card to red. He/she will have to suffer a consequence for disregarding the classroom rules and jeopardizing everyone's right to learn.

In order to redeem himself/herself, a meaningful consequence is key. I've tried different kinds: including a simple apology, extra homework and lunch detentions. All three failed. Apologies become words without weight after a while. Having to follow up on extra homework and marking it is too much to handle and I feel like it puts the burden on me rather then on the student. Lunch detentions are also difficult to keep track of because they usually don't take place the same day (at least not at my school) and are a real headache.

I've always been told "If you've got to take away something, don't take away the kids' recess. They need to run outside to release their energy and breathe some fresh air!" I agree with that; however, it appears to be the only immediate consequence that really matters and truly works. So for me, a red card equals no recess. Again, if something else works for your class, feel free to do as you please.

Rewarding students for good behavior is as equally important. This can be done as a class reward or an individual reward. I usually start with class rewards. I fix a target for the number of green cards remaining at the end of the day. The class votes on a group reward. It can be an extra recess, a class party, a picnic, a pizza lunch, watching a movie... Again, the reward must be meaningful to them. Involve your students in coming up with different ideas. When the target is reached, we celebrate!

An individual reward that's worked quite well is community work. I had a student that was repeatedly staying in for recess and I could tell he had stopped caring. So I threatened him with community work if he got a red card again. Of course, he did! I had him dust the window blinds and clean students' desks. This didn't seem like a punishment to him at all! He had the biggest smile on his face the whole time.

So I turned the situation around and told him that since he enjoyed helping out in the classroom so much, the next time he kept his green card he could choose to either go to recess or stay in to help clean up! That really worked for him. It made him feel good to contribute to the classroom by sorting our many toys into the right containers, neatly organizing our bookshelves, and washing the doorknobs in the hall, among other things. It also gave us the opportunity to chat a bit while he was doing his work, providing for some much needed attention and allowing us to know each other a little better.

Another year, I tried using the same strategy with a little boy but he really wasn't into cleaning... Instead, I told him he could choose to play in the classroom with a friend or go outside for recess whenever he kept his green card. It was surprisingly really successful and I tend to use that approach now with my little troublemakers!

In November, I change my reward incentive to individually reward students for their daily efforts. After a while, you quickly realize that the same students end up losing their red card and it's not fair for the whole class to lose out. I love giving away food treats (healthy food mostly) before kids go home. For instance, I'll buy a box of cheese crackers to share with everyone that was able to keep his/her green card until the end of the day. I do it every day and I change the food reward every week (I choose nut-free products): fruits, baby carrots, cereals, popcorn, marshmallows and oatmeal cookies are delicious healthy (for the most part) treats! It works wonders, believe me; students strive to behave and get their daily treat. They simply love it!

Whichever strategy you use, be consistent. Apply the rules until the class behaves to your expectations. Students should listen to your warnings carefully the first time without you having to repeat yourself or raise your tone to be understood, especially in September and October while they are getting accustomed to your routine and your teaching style. Don't allow students to argue with you. Use the broken record technique:

-No talking back!
-But...

-No talking back!
-Yes, but...
-No talking back!

When you know each other better, ease off a bit, but only as long as discipline problems have become the exception to the rule. Establishing a quiet environment should enable you to address your class without having to speak loudly. It will help you preserve healthy vocal cords and maximize your students' overall learning experience.

RULE #4: CELEBRATE!

Noise pollution is undeniably hazardous for your voice. For that reason, when the enemy is defeated it is extremely important to celebrate your victory. Often Compliment your class and kids individually on how quietly they listen, work and walk in the hall to boost their self-esteem and encourage them in the right direction.

I remember explaining my strategy during a job interview. The principal asked me, "Do you sometimes get complaints from parents about the strict way you teach students to remain quiet and stay still?" I answered, "Absolutely not because we make it a celebration!" Parents congratulate me for taking the time to teach their children the skills of self-control, focus and respect. They are grateful for the structure I provide and the positive results that ensue on their report cards.

The Silence Diet has to be perceived as a positive lifestyle. When you think of it, the Silence Diet has close ties with meditation techniques. One parent pointed that out to me and said that she and her son had taken this practice home and meditated similarly every night to improve his skills. It helped him tremendously on many levels. What a smart mom! She understood that slowing down the activities of the body builds a solid foundation on which to build.

In her book *Eat, Love, Pray*, Elizabeth Gilbert writes about Vipassana Meditation: "If I could sit through this non-lethal physical discomfort, then what other discomforts might I someday be able to sit through? What about emotional discomforts, which are even harder for me to endure? What about jealousy, anger, fear, disappointment, loneliness, shame, boredom?"[52] Many of these emotions are common in our little one's heart. They often are the reasons why they can't focus in class. As they are learning to cope with intense emotions for their first time, it is important to learn the ability to stop, reflect and control.

Noise awareness is so important that The League for the Center for Hearing and Communication dedicates an entire day to it. Every year, they solicit schools and communities to get involved in observing a full minute of silence between 2:15 and 2:16, regardless of location. In her 2007 press release, Amy K. Boyle, Director of Public Education in New York, states that *continuous exposure to noise above 85 decibels can be harmful to hearing and documented research has found noise does not have to be that loud to lead to physiological changes in blood pressure, sleep, digestion and other stress-related disorders. Studies exist documenting the harmful effects of noise on children's learning and behavior. "It is time," Boyle says, "that we take responsibility to quiet our surroundings and create a healthy environment for us and our children."* [53]

There are different ways to help promoting a quiet environment in your school. You can start by teaching a unit on noise and the threat it represents on hearing. Show how it affects one's behavior and learning capabilities. Measure and compare noise levels in different areas of your school: in the classroom, in the library, in the cafeteria, in the gym, in the hall, in the office... Organize a poster or a writing contest to illustrate

---

[52] Gilbert, Elizabeth. Eat, Pray, Love. New York, USA. Vikin Penguin, 2006, p. 174
[53] Boyle, Amy K. "Noise Center", Center for Hearing and Communication. 2010 Center for Hearing and Communication. October 10th, 2010. <http://www.chchearing.org/noise-center-home/international-noise-awareness-day/sample-press-release>

dangers associated with noise pollution and how it can be remedied. Be creative!

First, build up student's enthusiasm regarding the Silence Diet and the value of a quiet environment. Next, celebrate silence along with thousands of other schools with the International Noise Awareness Day. The League for the Hard of Hearing holds it every year. To honor silence, participants remain absolutely quiet and without making any noises between 2:15 p.m. and 2:16 p.m. on the day of the event. Visit The League for the Hard of Hearing's website for more information and to know when the next International Noise Awareness Day will take place at www.lhh.org.

CHAPTER SIXTEEN
Classroom Management

MORE ON MANAGEMENT

Great structure and consistent discipline provide for a peaceful classroom environment. This makes all the difference in the world when it comes to saving your voice and maximizing your students' learning experience. I want to share with you some more ideas that work for me and my students. If you're new to teaching, these might come handy. If not, feel free to skip this section.

NO TALKING BACK!

I've always been a calm child, submitting easily to whatever was expected of me. I rarely got in trouble. If I did, I'd explain what happened to my parents or teacher and they would explain to me where and why I was wrong. That was it. Reasoning worked for me. I trusted my parents' and teachers' opinion and I'd do as I was told. When I started teaching, I felt it was important to let students express themselves and give importance to their feelings and ideas. I still believe that. However, there are more appropriate times than others to do so.

At the beginning, I made the mistake of letting students explain themselves too much when I was trying to discipline them. That opened the way to arguing and power struggles. It was really exhausting and mentally unhealthy to argue with students. It gave them the wrong sense of control and the feeling that perhaps they could "get away with it this time" when I was the one supposed to make decisions and give consequences. One day, another teacher was nice enough to tell me that I shouldn't let students talk back to me whatsoever. I had not even realized this was happening. From the moment I stopped letting students make up excuses or give me attitude, things significantly improved.

It goes along with what I was saying earlier. Ask students: Who's the boss of your family? Mom and Dad. Who's the boss of the school? The principal. Who's the boss of the classroom? The teacher. Who's the boss of your body? YOU!

I worried that I might come across as a control freak witch; it's not the case. I do give students plenty of opportunities to express their feelings and ideas; however, during conflicts I am the one making decisions and my decisions are final. When students walk into my classroom, I want them to know this is a learning environment, not a battlefield. This setting allows students to positively and actively participate, and assimilate information effectively while enjoying themselves in a place where respect is not only expected, but required.

THE BROKEN RECORD TECHNIQUE

I briefly discussed this technique earlier... What can you do when students keep cutting you off with their "I didn't do it!", "He started it", "But...", or refuse to comply with your instructions? Use this simple but efficient strategy: repeat the exact same sentence until they stop arguing or stop whatever they are doing wrong. For example, say "Apologize to your friend!" Pause a couple of seconds and say it again until the student actually stops talking and apologizes to the other kid. If you want a student to stop rocking on his chair, say "Stop rocking on your chair." Wait for a bit and repeat it again until he or she surrenders to your request. The Broken Record Technique always works for me and it will for you, too. If it doesn't, you're not doing it properly!

WORKING IN THE CLASSROOM IS A PRIVILEGE.
In a classroom setting, it will often be the same students disrupting your lesson or preventing others from concentrating on their work. A child's desire for attention, positive or not, is ancient. Disciplining that child gives them their fix, and this is why consequences aren't always enough to bring a child back to common sense.

Also, a child that is constantly being disciplined stops caring. I've tried sending troublemakers to the office but it felt as if some students were actually looking forward to that because they got more attention from the principal and their parents, and mostly they often ended up not having to do work while they sat there waiting.

In the long run it backfired on me because it was interpreted as a reflection on my inability to manage my class. If this happens to you, remember that there always are more profound psychological reasons for children misbehaving on which, you and I don't have any control: for instance difficult family situations, poor physical and mental health and the way they were brought up. Sometimes, it's easier to blame the teacher rather than going through the painful process of facing and analyzing what makes a child so angry or emotionally unstable. Don't take it too much to heart and continue trying your best to help those children. They need your love.

I was very lucky that other more experienced teachers at my school noticed that I was struggling with my class. They offered to take those students in their classrooms so the rest of us could have a little peace during independent working time. It was a little embarrassing for them to go to younger grades or it was intimidating to be with older students.

Sometimes I had to remove some students even before the

actual lesson started and they missed the interactive parts of it. At those times, it seemed that some students always tried to ruin my fun activities, turning them into a chaotic experience instead, so I didn't take that chance. I'd send them to work with other teachers as soon as possible. They started to feel regret about missing explanations and advice. They were on their own. But that was part of the plan: to make them realize that being in my classroom was a privilege. The plan was for them to <u>want</u> to be in my classroom again and behave accordingly to stay. And it worked!

After a week or two, those students wanted to be part of my class so badly that they changed their behavior completely. It was difficult to explain this approach to the parents and principal and how these students would benefit in the end but ultimately, it worked to their advantage.

Today, when I see other teachers in my hall struggle with their kids, I always offer to take some of them in my classroom to work. I send my colleagues some kids too. We swap! It's nice to work as a team and feel that we can count on each other for support, and it sends the message that teachers are on the same page. That creates a sense of consistency and emphasizes what is acceptable in the school.

SHOW SOME TOUGH LOVE!

After a trip at the office, an accusation I heard on a couple occasions was "I behave that way because Mme. Bastien doesn't like me!" Putting blame on a teacher for responding to inappropriate behavior with discipline does not solve anything. In the past I have responded with: "It's not you that I don't like, it's your behavior!" Sometimes political correctness takes us away from the real issues at heart. When a student is repeatedly disrespectful or abusive to the teacher and other kids, it can make the teacher slowly start losing some of that unconditional love they should have towards students.

One of my teacher friends, Sheila Peytonn Neave from Georgia (USA), shared the following with me:

"I'm retired but I definitely believe that with the middle and high school kids I taught, voice is important. I don't believe in being all sweet and sugary when you're obviously displeased with something. It's dishonest; they don't go for it. I don't mean yelling, but there's a time and place for stern reprimand with teenagers. At the same time, they can tell if praise is genuine or just words. For example, the Boys Town model mandates that no matter how bad the behavior infraction, the teacher is supposed to keep the monotone candy-coated praise thing going first... The kids thought it was a joke and so did I!"

Teachers have feelings, too, and I think that it's important to express our emotions within reason. The core problem is that in being overly sweet despite the breach, the impression of being much too kind is given; a weakness kids interpret as untruthful and try to take advantage of. That kind of abuse is unacceptable. Bullying doesn't only take place in the schoolyard: students and parents bully teachers too. That is why we must set limits. Be kind to people and people will be kind in return.

The contrary is true as well. This is a basic principle that they can understand. Children are capable of recognizing that actions have specific repercussions. Ignoring that fact may do more harm than facing the truth. It's in that respect that we have to show tough love. In the long run, concealing our true emotions encourages students to disregard the effect their behavior has on people and on themselves. I continue to believe in being politely straightforward; and every time I tell a kid that respect was lost because of what was done, better positive choices to change the behavior are made. We are able to start anew and build on a respectful student-teacher relationship to progress on both personal and academic levels. Everybody wins.

There is some value in how to use your voice properly to convey that kind of message. To avoid charging it with any aggressiveness, make sure to use a medium pitch and place your voice in the mask—your natural resonators—as discussed earlier. Use a calm, confident and firm tone. The beauty of your voice will help appease the listener and make your student more receptive to the sincerity of your intentions. The tone and the words that you use are what matters the most. You can sound assertive and caring at the same time. After all, you wouldn't go through all that trouble if you didn't care, would you?

One last piece of advice regarding that approach: Explain to your principal that office support is important to you in these situations. That way, your principal will feel more involved and will more likely understand that you are acting strategically. They will respect you for reaching out and will back you up.

THE THREE MOST IMPORTANT THINGS TO LEARN

What's more important than reading, more important than writing and more important than counting? This is a question I ask my students the very first day of school in September and again and again throughout the year. The answer is:

1) Be kind. When you are kind, people are kind to you. You give joy and you feel joy. It makes everybody happy.

2) Use your common sense: If you use your common sense, you will know the difference between right and wrong. You will keep yourself out of trouble and safe.

3) Forgive one another for our mistakes. Sometimes, people forget to be kind and don't use common sense. Be accountable for your mistakes and forgiving for others so that we can all move on and start fresh. Every day is a new day.

This is fundamental to my teaching and lifestyle. These are values I genuinely believe in and that I feel give substance to one's character. At the end of the day, it's all about self-control; total control over the mind and body, and respect. These are crucial skills to succeed in life.

The next pages will bring about more personal insights on my teaching philosophy and how to use meditation in order to teach students how to concentrate, manage their feelings, and apply visualization techniques to boost their self-esteem and confidence.

CHAPTER SEVENTEEN
My Teaching Philosophy

Society puts enormous pressure on children to perform in school: from parents, teachers, from the children themselves, as well as peer pressure. Poor marks are often met with reprimands, loss of privileges at home, embarrassment and a vanishing self-esteem. With the rise of anxiety, one of the most fundamental principles of learning—"learning is fun"—is threatened. No wonder some students resent going to school. No wonder negative experiences become sour memories after reaching adulthood. A dangerous precedent is set when a parent cannot instill the love of learning in his or her child.

FEAR IS THE ENEMY!
Fear-based learning is stressful and inhibits children from reaching their full potential. In his book, *Effortless Mastery*, Kenny Werner writes: "a fearful mind won't allow you to concentrate and absorb."[54] I believe the solution to this is to annihilate all psychological barriers attached to learning difficulties. I'm making an allusion to negative connotations linked to the failure of a task or to long-term academic troubles. Clearly, parents and teachers all want their children and students to be successful.

But how is success defined? The school system specifically wants it to be reflected in B's and A's on report cards. Students failing to meet our society's expectations can result in academic

---

[54] Werner, Kenny. Effortless Mastery. New Albany, IN. Jamey Aebersold Jazz, Inc., 1996, p. 60

weaknesses being an embarrassment. To bypass this feeling, we sometimes resort to constantly complimenting kids on their work without taking quality into account.

Blame this on a recent trend that, in French, is referred to as the phenomenon of *l'enfant roi*. "Son king" is the literal translation; "spoiled brat" is close but too strong and not exactly what it symbolizes. I'm not sure if there really is an equivalent English expression that does justice to its true meaning. I translated the following passage written by Sylvie Halpern which appeared in an article that was published in the French-Canadian *Châtelaine* (September 2004) issue to help you understand better what it stands for: "The child is the heart of the adult's need for continuation; the passing on of genetic and family history. The adult cannot take the risk of demonstrating the slightest blame or dislike for the child in his or her eyes."[55]

How can a child better himself/herself without knowing where the problems lie? Kids are very smart. They often don't need an adult to confirm how they are doing. They generally can tell just by comparing themselves with their peers and making a judgment of their own. Sending a contradictory message is confusing.

Here is a suggestion on how to cope with that challenge. As illustrated in the article "Read Well (Bien Lire!)", try to "de-dramatize the situation. Sometimes, a teenager's difficulty to concentrate is amplified by his/her parents' anxiety."[56] Start off by explaining to children what our levels mean. Here in Ontario

---

[55] Halpern, Sylvie. "Vivre mieux : L'enfant roi", Châtelaine. September 2004 Rogers Media. October 10th, 2010.
<http://www.chatelaine.qc.ca/famille/article.jsp?content=20041108_164016_6516&page=2>

[56] Jung, Laurence. "Prévenir l'échec scolaire par une approche globale", Bien Lire! February 2005 CNDP. October 10th, 2010. <http://www.bienlire.education.fr/02-atelier/fiche.asp?theme=1110&id=1362>

(Canada), the Ministry of Education requires teachers to assess assignments using 1 to 4 levels; 4 corresponds to an A and 1 to a D. I often use the grid below to briefly explain to parents what the levels represent.

ASSESSMENT GRID

LEVELS	IN LETTERS	WHAT DOES IT MEAN?
Level 4	A- to A+	Excellent: student demonstrates understanding that goes beyond curriculum expectations.
Level 3	B- to B+	Satisfying: student meets curriculum expectations.
Level 2	C- to C+	Limited Understanding: student needs some teacher support in order to meet curriculum expectations.
Level 1	D- to D+	Very Limited Understanding: student needs extensive teacher support to meet curriculum expectations.

In order to convert the levels into a more simplistic language for kids, I use the ice cream cone imagery. I tell students that a B represents three ice cream scoops; they did the work correctly as expected with few mistakes. A C equals two ice cream scoops; the student needs help from the teacher to understand and complete the task at hand or there might be quite a few errors present. I give one ice cream scoop or a D to a student that doesn't quite understand what to do, doesn't complete the assignment despite teacher support, or has tremendous difficulty finishing the work. An A is the cherry on top! The child accomplishes the task easily with close to no mistake or impresses me by adding to my expectations with his/her own meaningful ideas for example by showing a higher learning level of understanding. You can build a visual reference to hang on the ceiling or post on your classroom walls like these ones:

I tell the kids that there is absolutely no shame in getting a C (two ice cream scoops) or a D (one ice cream scoop) unless this is the result of time unnecessarily wasted instead of doing work. There will be future opportunities to revisit what was missed and misunderstood in order to improve oneself. I explain how we are all different and that we cannot all have every talent. If one's strength is reading, the other's strength might be sport. Who's to say which is more valuable?

If a student has difficulty executing a task, awareness is essential to make things better. When one knows where weaknesses are, it's easier to better focus on difficulties and take up the challenges they represent. It can be quite distressful to have the feeling you're not doing as well as you should and not know where you went wrong. It's our job to tell the truth and accurately assess a performance. No secrets and above all, no lies. In my opinion, this is often a huge burden taken off a child's shoulders, particularly when parents understand and share that vision. Success can be defined by the extent of one's individual progress. If a student receives a D in September in Reading and another in June, that still goes to show how much a child has learned in the meantime!

I have strong convictions when it comes to how success versus failure should be viewed. I try to convey a message of perseverance. What's important for me is to see a child try his or her best. When faced with a challenging task, I want to see students answer questions to the best of their abilities. Fear paralyses. Again, how can one improve upon oneself without having tried in the first place? By getting out of their comfort zone and taking risks in answering questions, students have nothing to lose. A right answer is reassuring while a wrong answer is another opportunity to learn and become smarter. Nothing less, nothing more!

One day, a first grade student taught me a fantastic lesson on letting go of his fears. This happened at the end of a math activity on adding money values under $0.30. He came to me and asked if he could address the class. He said, "I didn't care if I got it right or wrong, I just tried my best!" Later in the afternoon, we were doing some individual reading in French (remember that this is a French Immersion class). That same student seemed upset and had not started to read yet. He told me it was too difficult to read and answer the questions both in French. I reminded him of the very same words he told me following our math lesson and that he should approach reading the same way. His face brightened up as he realized he'd better be consistent with what he had said earlier. Guess what; it worked! He finished the task on his own and it was very well done! This is what I learned: success is defined by one's mindset.

Another day, a second grade student was encouraging a fellow first grade classmate who appeared extremely hesitant to write in his journal. He told his friend "They're just words... They won't hurt you!" I interrupted everybody's work and I asked the boy to share that thought with the rest of the class. His remark inspired a little sketch in my mind and so we proceeded to a short improvisation in front of the class to illustrate his idea. I called it The Word Fight and it went like this:

THE WORD FIGHT

-Hey you, Word! *(Point at an imaginary word.)*

-Do you think you can scare me? *(Pretend to prepare for a fight.)*

-Come on... Come closer! *(Move fingers of your hand toward yourself invitingly.)*

-Come closer if you dare! *(Stomp your foot on "dare".)*

-Well, guess what?! *(Place your hands on your hips.)*
-I'm gonna WRITE YOU DOWN! *(Point your index finger down to imaginary piece of paper.)*

The class erupted into laughter! Not only did it break the tension in that young mind but it also made him realize that he had nothing to lose. As long as he tried, nothing wrong could happen. I often practice this sketch with my class when I see someone in a similar state of mind. I'll even change it up a little according to each situation. For example, I'll change "write you down" to "read you out". What it all comes down to is that when one tries his/her best, it only gets BETTER! For your convenience, I have included a complete lesson plan about The Word Fight at the end of this book.

LETTING THE EGO GO

Another concept widely explored in Werner's *Effortless Mastery* is how the ego prevents us from performing to the best of our capabilities. Werner defines the ego as "the lens through which we perceive our separateness from each other. Separateness invites comparison and competition. This is where problems originate: he's younger than I, more talented, and so forth."[57] Students really have to embrace the fact that they can't always be good at something the first time, every time and parents need to accept that their children are not perfect. In *Man's Search for Meaning*, the author Viktor E. Frankl uses his personal experience as a holocaust survivor to apply a technique called logotherapy: "Fear brings to pass what one is afraid of; likewise a forced intention makes impossible what one forcibly wishes."[58] That happens because of the anxiety and pressure desires and

---

[57] Werner, Kenny. Effortless Mastery. New Albany, IN. Jamey Aebersold Jazz, Inc., 1996, p. 52
[58] Frankl, Viktor E.. Man's Search for Meaning. New York, NY. Washington Square Press Publication of Pocket Books, 1959, p.145

excessive intentions paradoxically bring upon. To perform better, it is suggested to welcome failure and to not let it get to us. Stop being self-conscious!

Weaknesses should neither make one feel inferior nor should mistakes be underestimated and taken lightly. Balance and honesty are key to recognizing where there is room for improvement and acting upon it. Dissolving the ego and connecting with one's true self isn't that easy to do but it is doable even for children. It requires a certain force of character to build an imaginary shield around oneself and stop negative low self-esteem feelings associated with sadness, frustration, laziness, guilt, embarrassment, shame, vanity, jealousy, anger, to enter one's heart.

In a way, one has to become resilient and insensitive to critics to get better at a task. When the mind is free of psychological barriers, it is better prepared to concentrate and absorb knowledge. Students need to accept who they are and whatever comes to them in terms of learning skills with open arms, then, through perseverance, put forth the necessary efforts to conquer all their challenges. A blend of acceptance, hard work, patience and love is the recipe for success.

The good news is that with time and hard work progress always comes. I was watching the movie "Evan Almighty"[59] the other night and I would like to share with you my favorite quote: "If someone prays for patience, you think God gives them patience? Or does he give them the opportunity to be patient?" When teaching children or discussing with parents, I feel like children often expect themselves—or parents sometimes expect them—to be perfect on the first try. As a teacher, I see a parallel to this quote: that success or perfection cannot be gained instantly. It is *opportunities* leading to perfection that define who our students are and how successful they will

---

[59] Oederek, Steve. <u>Evan Almighty</u>. Universal Pictures. USA. June 22nd, 2007

become.   Understand   difficulties   and   weaknesses   as opportunities to learn and better yourself rather than fear the ego within.   I think it's wonderful to be able to provide learning opportunities to young souls and hopefully make a difference in their life. Isn't teaching the best job ever?!

CHAPTER EIGHTEEN
Meditation With Kids

A calm and focused class prevents you from raising the volume of your voice and consequently preserves your vocal cords. The quest for tranquility through meditation is yet another strategy I have found to help my students quiet down, allow me to teach and allow them to learn. So in addition to practicing being respectful from time to time, I often dive into an impromptu meditation with my students to help them release their stress and increase their self-confidence as young learners by focusing their mind.

When I close my eyes, a multitude of images and thoughts hit me, and I know it's the same for kids. It is very difficult to concentrate on one thought at a time for more than a few seconds. The mind is like a wild horse; however, with practice and perseverance it can be tamed. Why meditation you ask?

Not long ago, I read a popular folklore story called "Prince Five-Weapons".[60] In this story, a young prince graduates from his military service and is rewarded with a bow and arrows, a flacon of deadly poison, a sword, a spear and a club for weapons, along with the according title. As he is getting ready to cross the forest and return to his father's place, he is warned about a mean man-eating ogre named Sticky-Hair that lives there. Armed with his arsenal, Prince Five-Weapons fearlessly enters the forest. When they meet, Prince Five-Weapons soaks his arrow in the poison and shoots him. However, the arrow flies

---

[60] Campbell, Joseph. The Hero with a Thousand Faces. New York, NY. Princeton University Press, 1949, p. 85–87.

right into the ogre's sticky hair and unhurt; he shakes his head, making it fall to the ground. Prince Five-Weapons uses all of his weapons one by one to defeat the ogre, but all of them get stuck into the ogre's sticky hair. Finally, he last attempts to fight the ogre barehanded with a couple of punches to his face but instead both hands are drawn to the ogre's sticky hair. Before he knows it, his whole body is caught in the ogre's sticky hair. Prince Five-Weapons nevertheless keeps his composure.

The ogre is somewhat impressed by Prince Five-Weapons' tenacity and courage and he asks him, "Why are you not scared of me?" Prince Five-Weapons answers, "I have in my belly a thunderbolt for weapon. If you eat me, you will not be able to digest that weapon. It will tear your insides into tatters and fragments and will kill you. In that case we'll both perish. That's why I'm not afraid!"[61] Although it was a lie, the ogre believed him and, ravaged by the fear of dying, he gently put him down and let the prince continue on his journey.

In this story, the five weapons symbolize the convenience but marginality of the five senses and the body. What is more powerful is the invisible sixth sense: the mind and its knowledge. Using the mind alone, one can use all five senses to see, hear, smell, touch, taste and make a story silently come to life. Through a guided visualization, you can teach your students how to use their mind to set a positive mindset and reach their goals and realize their dreams.

In her book *Sensational Meditation for Children*, Sarah Wood Vallely explains that meditation is more than "wishful thinking, overcoming mental blocks and increasing mental acuity. It synchronizes our right and left-brain hemispheres' wave patterns. When these hemispheres are in sync with each

---

[61] Campbell, Joseph. <u>The Hero with a Thousand Faces</u>. New York, NY. Princeton University Press, 1949, p. 87

other they communicate better with one another, and therefore function with more clarity and focus."[62]

To tie this in with the matter of preserving your voice and answering the original question "Why meditation?" I believe that meditation leads to better self-control, better concentration, better work habits, better self-confidence, more creativity, more academic successes, less frustration, less classroom disruptions and it creates a classroom setting where you don't have to raise the loudness of your voice to be heard or to resolve issues.

CREATING MEDITATIONS FOR THE CLASSROOM

I generally don't tell my students that we are about to meditate or they might think I'm a little crazy and start acting silly! So if you, too, are a little turned off by the idea of meditating, please keep an open mind; it is a common misconception to believe that meditation is simply relaxation, or only for religious people. Nobody has to be spiritual to enjoy the benefits of meditation. And I don't have my students sit in a lotus position and say "Om!"

There is more to meditation than letting the mind go blank. I actually want quite the opposite. If you are still uncomfortable with the idea of meditating, simply view this as a concentration game or a visualization exercise aimed at developing one's imagination and increasing mindfulness. Also, you don't have to be an expert on meditation to help your students achieve a state of tranquility and unlock the power of their thoughts. Here are a few meditation examples you can use in your classroom as is or build on to create your own and adapt to specific situations and events occurring in your classroom. I've included questions to ask your class after a meditation to allow them to share their experiences. You will also find follow-up lesson plans at the end

---

[62] Wood Vallely, Sarah. Sensational Meditation for Children. Asheville, NC. Satya Method Resource Center, 2006, p.7

of this book, complete with follow-up activity ideas in order to make the time spent on these meditations relevant to teaching your curriculum.

MEDITATION #1: I'M AN EXCELLENT READER!

This is the first meditation I tried with my class and probably my favorite! I like doing it at the carpet right after we've practiced being respectful or before a reading activity. I do it with emergent readers to increase their positive image of themselves as readers and hopefully tear down any barriers the anxiety of reading sometimes creates. It can be adapted to other learning situations.

MEDITATION:

Sit comfortably, close your eyes, take a deep breath and slowly breathe out. Continue breathing slowly. Feel your body relax more and more with each new breath. Take a couple more breaths.

Imagine yourself walking in your bedroom. You left your backpack by your bed. Look in your schoolbag. You find your favorite book. This book is so much fun that you want to start reading it right away. You start reading the first page with confidence: "Once upon a time..." You are doing such a great job reading every word perfectly. Tell yourself, "I'm an excellent reader!"

Turn the page. You keep reading with amazing clarity and flow. You look up and you realize that you aren't alone in the room anymore. Your mom, your dad and your brothers and sisters heard you read so well that they came to listen. You keep reading the story effortlessly with enthusiasm. Reading is easy and fun for you. Your parents are listening very attentively because you are such an excellent reader! Yes, you are! Tell yourself: "I'm an excellent reader!"

You finished the book so you close it. Your family congratulates you on being such an excellent reader. You're happy because you can see how proud of you they are. That makes you feel proud. Tell yourself again: "I'm an excellent reader!" Hear your mom and dad ask you "how did you become such an excellent reader?" You answer, "I don't know. I guess it was always in me!" Yes, it feels good to know that you have the knowledge to read inside of you and that is why you are such an excellent reader! You did a fantastic job. Thank yourself for your hard work. You can now open your eyes.

SHARING QUESTIONS:
1. What did you see in your mind?
2. What did you sound like when you were reading?
3. How did your parents congratulate you?
4. How do you feel?

Feel free to vary the setting of this meditation from time to time. For example, ask students to imagine themselves reading for their reading buddy, you or another teacher, a classmate, or better yet, in front of the whole class! Instead of focusing on reading, the topic of this meditation could also revolve around being an excellent writer or an excellent communicator. The perfect follow-up activity for this meditation would be to have one of your students read a book for the class. Don't forget that a lesson plan for this meditation is available at the end of this book.

MEDITATION #2: THE BLOSSOMING TREE
"The Happy Tree",[63] a meditation written by Sarah Wood, inspired this visualization exercise. I came up with it on an early

---

[63] Wood Vallely, Sarah. Sensational Meditation for Children. Asheville, NC. Satya Method Resource Center, 2006, p. 112–114

spring afternoon, when my kids were allowed to go out for recess without their jackets on for the first time and they had come back extremely excited. This was simply a way to channel their energy into something positive and calming before doing our work.

MEDITATION:

Sit comfortably, close your eyes, take a deep breath and slowly breathe out. Continue breathing slowly. Feel your body relax more and more with each new breath. Take a couple more breaths.

Imagine that you are a tree. You stand tall on the ground and feel the warmth of the sun shining on your hundred branches. It is beautiful outside! Spring is here. The branches have tiny buds on them just about to come out. They are filled with excitement. What are these buds thinking? Ask a bud, "How are you doing today? Why are you so excited?" Now, ask the bud if it needs anything and how you can help with that. Give the bud what it needs. Watch the bud blossom into the most beautiful flower you have ever seen. Admire every bud blossoming into hundreds of gorgeous flowers.

Tell yourself, "These are the most beautiful flowers I have ever seen!" And that's not all: these gorgeous flowers have a fantastic perfume too! There is a soft breeze bringing the smell of fresh grass and tulips growing nearby. Hear the birds singing as they fly above surveying the area to nest. It smells, feels and looks like spring and that is simply wonderful! You did a great job! Thank yourself for your great work. You can now open your eyes.

SHARING QUESTIONS:
1. What did you see in your mind?
2. Why was the bud so excited?

3. What did the bud need to transform into the most beautiful flower you have ever seen?
4. What did the most beautiful flower you have ever seen look like?
5. How do you feel?

This meditation can be used as a drama activity. It can be done seated or standing up. For example, ask your students to stand with their arms wide open and act out (hands to themselves and keeping their eyes closed if possible) what happens in the story. It could also work to play a recording of new age music with birds singing in it if you have any.

In the original "Happy Tree" meditation, the tree has fruits instead of buds. Some of the fruits are happy and some are sad. The tree asks the fruits why they feel that way and how to make the sad fruits feel better. To channel some of the energy that this meditation evokes, it might be a good idea to have students write in a journal entry, about what the buds or fruits needed, especially if adapted with a stronger emotional component. You can see the potential this story has to offer. A detailed lesson plan is provided at the end of this book.

MEDITATION #3: BUBBLE-MAKING IN THE FOREST!

Kids are generally very sensitive beings and sometimes don't know how to let go of negative feelings. I like to use this visualization to help kids cope with anxiety and stressful situations in their lives.

MEDITATION:

Sit comfortably, close your eyes, take a deep breath and slowly breathe out. Continue breathing slowly. Feel your body relax more and more with each new breath. Take a couple more breaths.

It's a beautiful afternoon. Imagine that you are walking in the forest. It feels really peaceful to hear the wind blowing through shimmering leaves. There is a small bottle of bubbles right in the middle of the trail. Pick it up. Open it. Dip the bubble blowing tube into the solution and gently blow a huge bubble. Watch the shiny bubble gently take flight in the blue sky. Blow another one. And another one. They are equally pretty in the sunshine.

Wait! Something is taking shape inside of each bubble! It's you! In each bubble, you see your reflection accomplishing something. Each bubble is like a mini movie screen and you're watching your life playing inside. In one bubble, you're having dinner with your parents. In the other one, you're playing outside with your friends during recess. What else do you see? Some of the bubbles might have happy stories in them and others might have sad stories too but it's o.k. Let the bubbles that make you feel sad or angry burst either on their own or against the tree branches so that only the happy bubbles survive and float around you.

Continue blowing more bubbles. Watch the happy bubbles swirl up around you. Feel yourself becoming as light as the bubbles; so light that your feet start lifting from the ground. Feel your feet leave the ground. You are now flying in the majestic blue sky surrounded by all your happy bubbles. You were very good at blowing bubbles; fantastic job! Thank yourself for such a fun time. You can now open your eyes.

SHARING QUESTIONS:

1. What did you see in each bubble?

2. Tell me about your happy bubbles.

3. Were you able to let go of the sad bubbles?

4. How do you feel?

It would be fun to replicate this meditation in real life and go outside to blow bubbles on that day or the next. Buy some bubble making wands and mix at your local Dollar Store. If you choose to repeat this lesson the following year, re-use the wands and make your own bubble solution. Mix one-part liquid dish soap to fifteen parts water. Hand soap doesn't work as well. Also beware of dish soap that contains anti-foaming ingredients!

This activity can be tied in with a math lesson in geometry, measuring, data management and probability. Imagine the possibilities! Refer to the lesson plan at the end of this book for complete instructions.

MEDITATION #4: THE GIFT

The Gift is a great meditation to develop faith in oneself and in one's future. When people ask me "What do you believe in?" I answer, "I believe in ME!" It doesn't matter what your religious beliefs are because God, or whatever supernatural power you believe in, put us on this earth and lives in each one of us. It is a very empowering feeling to know that the greatest power resides in ME and the only way to make things happen is to make them happen MYSELF. It starts with optimistic thinking. It starts with positive waves of energy attracting what I want for my future and myself. It is all about the power of vibrations. This meditation was created with the help of renowned speaker and hypnotherapist Matt Adams and Jaime Vendera's Vocal Mindset[64].

MEDITATION:

Sit comfortably, close your eyes, take a deep breath and slowly breathe out. Continue breathing slowly. Feel your body relax

---

[64] Adam, Matt & Vendera, Jaime. "Vocal Mindset", Just for Singers; This is Your World. October 10th, 2010. <http://www.justforsingers.com/Jaime-Vendera.php>

more and more with each new breath. Take a couple more breaths.

Imagine that you're a little early for school and that you are the first one to arrive at your classroom. The door is wide open and from where you are standing, you can see your desk. Hey! Guess what you see right on top of your desk: a gift! This present is beautifully wrapped. That's not all... It says your name on it in big letters! So you decide to walk in the classroom to check it out a little more closely.

You open the box. Wow! Today is your lucky day because in the box is everything you ever wanted! What do you want in life? What do you aspire to be in life? Think about what you want to find in your box (encourage kids to come up with a meaningful wish as opposed to something materialistic). Complete the following sentence in your mind: I want _____. Imagine your wish coming true and how it feels. Now believe that it is happening. Repeat in you mind, "I'm in the process of realizing my dearest dream of _____." You feel very excited and blessed that in the box is everything you ever wanted. That is such an amazing gift! But you know what? You deserve it! Thank yourself for such a cool and wonderful gift. You can now open your eyes.

SHARING QUESTIONS:
1. What did you see in your gift?

2. How did it make you feel to receive all you ever wanted?

3. What do you have to do to make your dreams come true?

This is one of my favorite meditations and it should be repeated often. To attract what is wanted in life, one can repeat those three steps as often as needed: ask, feel, and believe. If a negative thought appears, a positive one should replace it, or the negative might be attracted to you. I like to follow this mediation with an integrated Visual Arts, Languages and Mathematics (Geometry) lesson in which each student builds his or her own box with construction paper. I bring fancy wrapping paper and shiny ribbons to school for students to decorate the gifts with. We add sparkles and feathers to personalize each box and make them unique and fun! Then, students write down what their dream is on a piece of paper with an action plan to put in the precious boxes! In the week that follows, I have a couple of students at a time show off their gift and talk to the class about their dearest dream. It is important to allow students the right to pass if not comfortable to share what might for some be very personal. If you are restricted with time, simply have everyone put their dream and action plan together in a single box.

Lesson plans for these meditations are organized in the last section of this book for your easy convenience.

Writing this book has been a fun rewarding journey for me. I love sharing and I hope the information you read in here was useful to you. You will find all the lesson plans I have been referring to at the end of this book for your easy reference. I am also including them in a FREE printable Voice Yourself Teacher Resources Guide available on my website. To download it, go to: www.voiceyourselfintheclassroom.com.

With this book, my goal has been to inspire you to develop healthy voice habits in order to maximize the inner beauty that resides in your soul and channel it through your voice. Always remember that speaking and singing come from a natural place. Give yourself some time to assimilate your new knowledge and see results. Patience and consistency are vital. You should never feel any discomfort when trying to find your natural dynamic speaking or singing voice and practicing your vocal placement. If you feel your voice, you are doing something wrong! Speaking should be graceful and uncomplicated. Sometimes, less is more, therefore always maintain balance in your approach to using your voice correctly and use common sense to find out what works best for you.

You are an integral part of the universe and the voice is one of so many wonderful God given gifts that you can utilize to become your most amazingly incredible self. Please apply the techniques suggested in this book and watch your voice shine. Watch your confidence rise. Watch your students respond positively to your new voice and mind-set. Watch your frustrations give way to peace. Feel the joy! Feel invincible!

I believe that thoughts become things. Every belief, every feeling, every emotion and action set the mood for your interactions with people and how your future unfolds. The voice being the carrier of so many of these things, imagine its power in the world! There is room for you and your voice to complete the equation of success in your life. This is what I see for you. Thank you for embarking on this journey with me. I wish you all the best; you can do it! Love your voice and be happy. Voice yourself!

Keep me informed of your progress, contact me if you need clarification on the voice exercises or any other topics discussed in this book, and send me your feedback! I am always available for private consultations as well. Contact me at: voiceyourselfintheclassroom@gmail.com

Sincerely,

APPENDIX
Useful Information and Documents

Lesson Plans

NATURAL DYNAMIC VOICE PLACEMENT EXERCISES	
Lesson Plan	
Grades	Primary, junior or high school if adapted.
Number of students	Works for any small or large group
Goal	Encourage students to develop healthy voice habits.
Subject Integration	This lesson is directly related to the Arts; specifically Drama and Dance.
Expectations Adapted from the Ontario Curriculum, Grades 1-8[65]	Demonstrate some basic elements of Drama and Dance such as appropriately changing and sustaining the tone of voice, quality and volume to convey feelings when role-playing.
Teacher Resources	None
Student Resources	None

Parts of the Lesson	Time	Lesson Description
Warm-Up	5 minutes	Advise the class that you will be teaching them how to place their speaking voice correctly without hurting their vocal cords. Discuss briefly why they think their voice is precious and why it should be cared for. Ask your class to stand up and spread out in the classroom where they have enough room to move their arms freely.

---

[65] "The Ontario Elementary Curriculum Documents", Ontario Ministry of Education, 2010 Queen's Printer for Ontario. October 10th, 2010.
<http://www.edu.gov.on.ca/eng/curriculum/elementary/>

FOLLOW-UP ACTIVITY		
Introduction	Deep Breathing and Support	
	5-10 minutes	<u>Breathing and Supporting Your Breath Correctly</u> • Breathe by the nose • Let your belly come out • Lay down on the ground with a book on your belly and watch it rise and fall • Practice deep breathing. Stand up straight, roll your shoulders back and lean slightly on the ball of your feet. • Raise up your arms while you inhale, and bring them down while you exhale • Smell a beautiful flower • Put your arms on your hips to feel your front and back lower ribs • Blow candles on a birthday cake • Imagine the syringe for your support • Squats
		<u>Keeping Your Tongue and Larynx Relaxed during Elocution</u> • Yawn loudly with arm gesture • Say "huh" • Say "la" • Drop the jaw until you feel your jawbone backing off under your earlobes • Gently press with the palms of your hands underneath your cheekbones to release tension • Yawning again , say "huh" and "la"

Application	Placing the Voice Into Its Natural Resonators:	
	10-15 minutes	Make Your Sound Travel • Pretend to be a witch or a duck (find your nasal voice)! • Pinch your nose • Move the voice up from the nose until the voice doesn't change when you pinch your nose again • Move the voice from there to the forehead, the top of the head, and the back of the head, between the ears and in the throat.
		From A Nasal Voice To The Right Placement • Pretend to be a witch or a duck (find your nasal voice)! • Pinch your nose • Move the voice up from the nose until the voice doesn't change when you pinch your nose • Say the alphabet, pinching your nose constantly to verify the correct placement of your voice
		Leaning Forward • Grab some easy reading material • Lean forward and read • Stand up straight slowly and carefully without moving the focus of your voice
		Pushing Your Breastbone or Chest • Make a fist with one hand and grasp it with the other • Hold a note on "ah" • Press quickly but against your chest • Pretend to be Tarzan!

	10 minutes	**Stick Your Tongue Out!** • Take a big breath • Stick your tongue out • Hold any note on "ah"
		Pitching Above the Pencil • Hold a pencil horizontally in your mouth (a clean straw or Popsicle stick would do better in a real classroom environment) • Say "ah" • Pitch the sound above the pencil
		Brrr • Close your eyes • Imagine a cold winter night • Say "brrr" expressively a few times • Add "I'm cold" • Say "brrr" several times and repeat different sentences in between
		Umm-hmmm • Tell the class they have to answer all your questions positively with "umm-hmmm" • Ask a bunch of questions • Count from 1 to 10 saying "umm-hmmm" in between numbers
		Have A Good Laugh! • Laugh loudly on "ah" • Pretend to be Santa Claus! • Count or say the alphabet while laughing
Consolidation	5-10 minutes	If you can sing a song together, invite your class to do a few scales with you or simply slide up and down on any given note using the lip bubbles and "Umm-hmmm" exercises for instance.

REFLECTIONS		
Effectiveness of lesson	5 minutes	-It's a good idea to ask volunteers to demonstrate for the class how well they're doing throughout the lesson. -Come back to the notion of voice placement being and excellent way to beautify one's voice and preserve it. -Ask students what they learned: what exercise was the funniest, difficult, easiest, worthwhile, et cetera.
Assessment		Base assessment on participation.
Reinvestment		Repeat this lesson as needed.

VOCAL WARM-UP EXERCISES		
Lesson Plan		
Grades		Primary, junior or high school if adapted.
Number of students		Works for any small or large group, hopefully no more than 35 students.
Goal		Encourage students to develop healthy voice habits
Subject Integration		This lesson is directly related to the Arts; specifically to Drama.
Expectations Adapted from the Ontario Curriculum, Grades 1-8[66]		Demonstrate some basic elements of Drama such as appropriately changing and sustaining the tone of voice, quality and volume to convey feelings when role-playing.
Teacher Resources		None
Student Resources		None
Parts of the lesson	**Time**	**Lesson Description**
Warm-Up	5 minutes	Advise the class that you will be teaching them how to warm-up their speaking voice correctly without hurting their vocal cords. Explain briefly how warming-up will slightly raise the body temperature to increase the flexibility of the muscles and cartilages involved in the speech process. Ask the class to come up with different situations where they would be required to speak loud and when warming-up their voice could come in handy. Ask your class to stand up and spread out in the room where they have enough space to move their arms freely.

---

[66] "The Ontario Elementary Curriculum Documents", <u>Ontario Ministry of Education</u>, 2010 Queen's Printer for Ontario. October 10th, 2010.
<http://www.edu.gov.on.ca/eng/curriculum/elementary/>

FOLLOW-UP ACTIVITY		
Introduction	Deep Breathing and Support	
	5-10 minutes	Warm-up #1: Deep Breathing • Stand-up straight • Breathe by the nose • Raise your arms up while you inhale and down while you exhale.
Application	Placing the Voice Into Its Natural Resonators:	
	10 -15 minutes	Warm-up #2: Consonants That Are Good For Your Belly! • Take a deep breath • Exhale on "sss", "fff", "vvv", "jjj" or "zzz" five times • Exhale on "sss", pause, "sss", pause, et cetera, five times
		Warm-up #3: Water Gargle • Take in some water in your mouth • Breathe deeply by your nose • Gargle five times *If you are planning on doing this lesson plan with your class, you might want to skip this part as it might lead to possible mischievous unwanted behaviors!
		Warm-up #4: Lip Bubbles • Take a deep breath • Do the lip bubbles sliding up and down throughout your entire range five times
		Warm-up #5: Lip Bubble Variations • Take a deep breath • Choose a pitch in the middle of your range and do the lip bubbles on it. Slide down on "ah" or "eh" five times
		Warm up #6: Tongue Trills • Inhale slowly through your nose • Roll an Italian "R" on any pitch five times

	5-10 minutes	**Warm-up #7: The Vocal Cord Stretch** • Inhale slowly through your nose • Slide up and down your register, singing on "ah" or "eh"
		Warm-up #8: Your Classroom Lingo • Breathe deeply • Practice your top ten sentences preceding each of them with ""umm-hmmm" If you do this with your class, have students come up with sentences they often use and practice them!
Consolidation		If you can sing, invite your class to do a few scales with you and sing a song.
REFLECTIONS		
Effectiveness of Lesson	5 minutes	-It's a good idea to ask volunteers to demonstrate for the class how well they're doing throughout the lesson. -Come back to the notion of when is it most useful to warm-up the vocal cords. -Ask students what they learned: what exercise was the funniest, difficult, easiest, worthwhile, et cetera.
Assessment		Base your assessment on participation.
Future Reinvestment		Repeat this lesson as needed.

BEING RESPECTFUL	
Lesson Plan	
Grades	Primary and junior
Number of students	Works for any small or large group, hopefully no more than 35 students.
Goals	Develop self-control to apply the notion of respect in the classroom and create a quiet and positive learning environment.
Subject Integration	This lesson is directly related to Social Studies (Heritage and Citizenship as per the Ontario Curriculum) as it teaches valuable skills on how to interact with others, specifically during class. It makes students aware that citizen responsibilities and self-control affect the teacher's right to teach and one's right to learn.
Expectations	Teach students to remain quiet and stay still during teaching time in order to eliminate disruptive noises and create a pleasant classroom atmosphere. It is preferable to start doing this lesson within the first week of September to clearly establish your expectations. This activity can be done as often as necessary afterwards. You can use it at the beginning of any lesson to help students settle down or sporadically to continue maintaining the skills.
Teacher Resources	A timer
Student Resources	None

Parts of the lesson	Time	Lesson Description
Warm-Up	5-10 minutes	Initiate a group discussion as to what it means to be respectful in the classroom during teaching/learning time. Lead the conversation towards describing what ideal circumstances you are looking for in order to maximize one's learning capabilities.
PART I		
Introduction	5 minutes	Explain to the class that they must learn self-control in order to remain quiet and stay still during teaching/learning time. This is what they must do:

		When sitting at the carpet students:
		    a) sit up straight
		    b) cross their legs
		    c) lace their hands on their laps
		    d) remain quiet

Application	1-10 minutes	Set the timer to one minute. Students must remain quiet and stay still until the timer reaches zero. Pause the timer every time someone lacks self-control by talking, moving their hands, moving their legs, et cetera. Only start the timer again when everybody is quiet and in position.
Consolidation		Congratulate students when the timer reaches zero and beeps. Let everybody silently applaud (without hands touching each other or raising hands in the air to preserve calm) or let students give themselves a pat on the shoulder for their good work!

PART II		
Introduction	5 minutes	Explain that you will continue to practice self-control and being respectful in different ways throughout the day. You can do the following exercise right away or later in the day.
		Repeat this activity when students are sitting at their desk. They must: a) sit up straight with their chair pushed in b) keep both knees under their desk c) lace their hands on their desk (where you can see them) d) remain quiet
Application	1-10 minutes	Set the timer to one minute. Students must remain quiet and stay still until the timer reaches zero. Pause the timer every time someone lacks self-control and talks, moves their hands, swings their feet, et cetera. Only start the timer again when everybody is quiet and in position.
Consolidation		Congratulate students when the timer reaches zero and beeps. Let everybody silently applaud (without hands touching each other or raising hands in the air to preserve calm) or let students give themselves a pat on the shoulder for their good work!

PART III		
Introduction	5 minutes	Explain again that you will continue to practice self-control and being respectful in different ways throughout the day. You can do the following exercise right away or later in the day.
		Practice this activity when students circulate in the hall. They must… a) line up (assigning spots to younger students avoids many arguments) b) put one finger on their mouth while raising the other one in the air. I like this because it gives me a great visual of who's ready and I then can give those students high fives for being so fast and respectful. This works well for primary students. You might have to let this one go for junior levels! c) remain quiet
Application	1-10 minutes	Set the timer to one minute. Circulate in line around the school. Students must remain quiet until the timer reaches zero. Stop walking and pause the timer every time someone lacks self-control and talks. Only start the timer again when everybody is quiet and in position.
Consolidation		Congratulate students when the timer reaches zero and beeps. Let everybody silently applaud (without hands touching each other or raising hands in the air to preserve calm) or let students give themselves a pat on the shoulder for their good work!

REFLECTIONS		
Effectiveness of Lesson	5 minutes	-Emphasize how well your students did and how impressed you were that they showed so much self-control and respect. -If students had a hard time doing the exercises, be specific as to how you would like them to improve and set a goal for next time. For example, reach zero in less than 10 minutes. -Ask the class why it worked or didn't work. -Ask the class how self-control and being respectful will help them learn (lead conversation towards the fact that it will facilitate their ability to concentrate).
Assessment		Use some of your observations in assessing student learning skills on report cards. For instance, this could easily reflect under independent work (whether students need teacher prompting to keep their self-control) cooperation with others, class participation and even goal setting to improve work or oneself in this case. A student that remains quiet and stays still during teaching/learning time demonstrates excellent aptitudes in all those categories.
Future Reinvestment		Repeat any part of this lesson often. It helps students settle down and concentrate by creating a calm environment. It's excellent to start the day, as they come back from recess, or before a test.

The Word Fight Lesson Plan	
Grades	Primary, junior or high school if adapted
Number of students	Works for any small or large group, hopefully no more than 35 students.
Goals	This is a feel good activity to help students gain self-confidence and annihilate anxiety of performance when it comes to writing and reading depending on the adaptation.
Subject Integration	This lesson is directly related to Drama and Languages. Please note that it can be applied to other strands if adapted to focus on other subjects.
Expectations Adapted from the Ontario Curriculum, Grades 1-8[67]	Interpret and communicate ideas and feelings and generate ideas and information to write for an intended purpose or audience.
Teacher Resources	None
Student Resources	None

---

[67] "The Ontario Elementary Curriculum Documents", Ontario Ministry of Education, 2010 Queen's Printer for Ontario. October 10th, 2010.
<http://www.edu.gov.on.ca/eng/curriculum/elementary/>

Parts of the lesson	Time	Lesson Description
Warm-Up	5 minutes	Tell the class that they are going to interpret a short skit on overcoming obstacles associated with writing.
Introduction	5 minutes	Ask students to tell you what challenges they encounter when writing.
Application	5 minutes	Have the class stand up (you can invite a couple of volunteers at the front with you) and have students repeat and act out each sentence of the skit after you. Here it is again: **The Word Fight** -Hey you, Word! *(Point at an imaginary word.)* -Do you think you can scare me? *(Pretend to prepare for a fight.)* -Come on… Come closer! *(Move fingers of your hand toward yourself invitingly.)* -Come closer if you dare! *(Stomp your foot on "dare".)* -Well, guess what?! (Place your hands on your hips.) -I'm gonna WRITE YOU DOWN! (Point your index finger down to imaginary piece of paper.)
Consolidation	5 minutes	Invite a few students at a time to perform the skit for the class.

REFLECTIONS		
Effectiveness of Lesson	5 minutes	Ask students: despite the humorous side of the skit, what is the message hidden in the fight analogy of this skit? What does it teach?
Assessment		Base assessment on class participation
Future Reinvestment		Whenever you see a student being overwhelmed or anxious with a task, interrupt the class and repeat that skit adapting it to the specific situation.

I'M AN EXCELLENT READER!	
Lesson Plan	
Grades	Primary, junior or high school if adapted.
Number of students	Works for any small or large group, hopefully no more than 35 students.
Goals	Encourage students to develop their reading or writing skills. Eliminate the stress associated with reading in front of other people and making inferences.
Subject Integration	This lesson is directly related to Languages, specifically the strand of Reading. Please note that it can be applied to other strands if the original meditation is adapted to focus on Writing or Oral Communication instead of Reading.
Expectations Adapted from the Ontario Curriculum, Grades 1-8[68]	Read short, written materials using phonics, knowledge of words and cueing systems to read fluently.
Teacher Resources	Classroom library
Student Resources	None

Parts of the lesson	Time	Lesson Description
Warm-Up	10 minutes	This part of the lesson includes the actual meditation and the after meditation questions of <u>Meditation #1: I'm an Excellent Reader!</u>

---

[68] "The Ontario Elementary Curriculum Documents", <u>Ontario Ministry of Education</u>, 2010 Queen's Printer for Ontario. October 10th, 2010.
<http://www.edu.gov.on.ca/eng/curriculum/elementary/>

FOLLOW-UP ACTIVITY		
Introduction	5 minutes	Choose a student to read a book, a poem or his/her own story (from a previous written assignment for example) to the class. If you have been working on a class novel, ask a student to read a few pages from that novel.
Application	5-20 minutes	Support the student with his/her reading if required and encourage him/her to think aloud about the story that he/she is reading in order to make inferences.
Consolidation	10 minutes	Tell your student: "You're an excellent reader!" Ask students to offer positive comments or ask questions about the book that was read to them.
REFLECTIONS		
Effectiveness of Lesson	5 minutes	Emphasize how well your student did and how impressed you were with his/her reading skills. Point out a few specific strengths. Offer constructive criticism as to how you would like to see your student improve and set a goal for his/her next reading.
Assessment		Base your assessment on fluency and cognitive skills.
Future Reinvestment		Repeat this lesson until every student had a chance to read for the class.

THE BLOSSOMING TREE		
Lesson Plan		
Grades	Primary, junior or high school if adapted.	
Number of students	Works for any small or large group, hopefully no more than 35 students.	
Goals	Reflect on an exciting moment of one's life to develop writing and higher thinking skills in dealing with positive emotions.	
Subject Integration	This lesson is directly related to Languages, specifically the strand of Writing and the learning skills of resolving conflicts and cooperation.	
Expectations Adapted from the Ontario Curriculum, Grades 1-8[69]	Generate, gather and organize ideas to write short materials. Edit and revise written work according to grade requirements.	
Teacher Resources	None	
Student Resources	Notebook, pencil and eraser	
Parts of the lesson	Time	Lesson Description
Warm-Up	10 minutes	This part of the lesson includes the actual meditation and the after meditation questions of Meditation #2: The Blossoming Tree.

---

[69] "The Ontario Elementary Curriculum Documents", Ontario Ministry of Education, 2010 Queen's Printer for Ontario. October 10th, 2010.
<http://www.edu.gov.on.ca/eng/curriculum/elementary/>

FOLLOW-UP ACTIVITY		
Introduction	5 minutes	Ask students to reflect on a past or future event that they are excited about or something sad if the meditation is adapted accordingly.
Application	20-30 minutes	Ask students to write a journal entry to explain what the event is and why it is making them feel that way.
Consolidation	15 minutes	Ask a few volunteers to share their journal entry with the class.
REFLECTIONS		
Effectiveness of Lesson	5 minutes	Emphasize how well the student did and how much fun the event sounds like or show empathy in the case of a sad event. Point out a few specific strengths in his/her journal entry. Offer constructive criticism as to how you would like to see your student improve his/her journal entry and set a goal for next time.
Assessment		Base your assessment on the quality of ideas offered, how they were organized and the application of language conventions appropriate for that grade.
Future Reinvestment		Repeat this lesson before or after the Holidays and if something special, such as a field trip, is coming up.

BUBBLE MAKING IN THE FOREST

Lesson Plan

Grades	Primary, junior or high school if adapted.
Number of students	Works for any small or large group, hopefully no more than 35 students.
Goals	Make connections with daily life activities, solving mathematical problems, represent and communicate results of an investigation.
Subject Integration	This lesson is directly related to Mathematics: specifically the strands of Geometry, Measuring and Data Management.
Expectations Adapted from the Ontario Curriculum, Grades 1-8[70]	Understanding geometrical properties in the real world, measure the diameter of a circle or the volume of a sphere with a traditional or a non-traditional unit according to grade level, collect, organize and display data in graphs.
Teacher Resources	Bubble making solution Bubble-blowing wands (1 per student) Bristol boards
Student Resources	Math notebook, measurement tape, ruler or timer, pencil and eraser

Parts of the lesson	Time	Lesson Description
Warm up	10 minutes	This part of the lesson includes the actual meditation and the after meditation questions of <u>Meditation #3: Bubble Making in the Forest</u>.

---

[70] "The Ontario Elementary Curriculum Documents", <u>Ontario Ministry of Education</u>, 2010 Queen's Printer for Ontario. October 10th, 2010.
<http://www.edu.gov.on.ca/eng/curriculum/elementary/>

FOLLOW-UP ACTIVITY		
Introduction	5 minutes	Let students know that the class will be going outside for a fun bubble-making and math measuring activity.
Application	25 minutes	Take the class outside and instruct students to measure the approximate diameter or to calculate the volume of 10 different bubbles by referring to their shadow on the ground, using a traditional or a non-traditional unit according to grade level, or to measure the bubbles' lifespan with a timer. Advise students to write down their results in their math notebook.
	30 minutes	Bring the class back to the classroom. In team or individually according to your preferences, ask students to organize and display their results in a graph using a Bristol board.
Consolidation	15 minutes	Display students' graphs on the walls. Compare results and discuss what the smallest and biggest diameters were.
REFLECTION		
Effectiveness of Lesson	5 minutes	Congratulate your student for their excellent work. Ask them how challenging it was to measure the bubbles and what other feedback they have on this activity.
Assessment		Class participation or graphs.
Future Reinvestment		Some kids might ask you to blow bubbles again at recess or on a warm June afternoon!

THE GIFT Lesson Plan	
Grades	Primary, junior or high school if adapted
Number of students	Works for any small or large group, hopefully no more than 35 students.
Goals	This is a feel-good activity to help students believe in themselves and to encourage them to take action in order to pursue their dreams.
Subject Integration	This lesson is directly related to Health, specifically the strands of Growth and Development in regards to developing values related to identity and relationships as lifelong processes. The follow-up activity integrates Languages, Visual Arts and Mathematics (Geometry).
Expectation	Create alignment between inner drives and outer expression. Use speaking skills and strategies appropriately to communicate feelings and ideas on different topics. Produce art works in a variety of traditional three-dimensional forms that communicate feelings and ideas using elements, principles, and techniques of visual arts. Construct three-dimensional shapes.
Teacher Resources	A beautifully wrapped gift with a lid that can be opened and closed easily without wrecking it.
Student Resources	A piece of paper A pencil Construction paper Wrapping paper Ribbons, feathers, sparkles, etc...

Parts of the lesson	Time	Lesson Description
Warm-Up	10 minutes	This part of the lesson includes the actual meditation and the after meditation questions of <u>Meditation #4: The Gift</u>.
FOLLOW-UP ACTIVITY		
Introduction	5 minutes	Show your beautiful gift box to the class or have students build their own. Explain that each student is going to contribute his/her "Everything I Ever Wanted" to the box.
Application	25 minutes	Ask students to describe their "Everything I Ever Wanted" on a piece of paper and to make a list of at least three things they should do to make their wish come true.
Consolidation	15 minutes	Invite students to put their "Everything I Ever Wanted" paper in the gift box. Welcome students to share what they wrote with the class only if they feel comfortable to do so.
REFLECTION		
Effectiveness of Lesson	5 minutes	Wish everybody good luck on pursuing their bliss and encourage them to commit themselves to the things they wrote. Ask students what they learned about each other or themselves during that lesson.
Assessment		Class participation
Future Reinvestment		Repeat this activity at different times of the year since students wishes may have come true or have changed.

Glossary

A

Acidic, acidifying: said of food with a bitter taste or that will increase acid production in the stomach during digestion. A pH lower than 7.

Air Pressure System: Composed of the trachea, lungs, chest muscles, diaphragm and abdominal muscles, they control how much air is taken into the body and released back out during inhalation and exhalation.

Alkaline, alkalizing: the opposite of acidic and acidifying. A pH higher than 7.

Air Purifier: small appliance that cleans the ambient air by eliminating allergens, viruses and other pollutants.

Antihistamine: an active ingredient in over-the-counter medications sold to stop the release of histamine in the blood in order to help the immune system fight against allergies.

B

Bacterial infection: sometimes contagious disease caused by a bacterium. Bacterial infections require the use of antibiotics to be annihilated.

Bel Canto: Italian vocal technique originating in the 17th century that emphasizes effortless singing and a beautiful tone. It means "beautiful singing"!

Breath Control: the power to make the most of one breath through endurance or the intensity and timing at which it is released.

Breath Support: coordination of the diaphragm and abdominal muscles controlling the pressure at which the air is inhaled and exhaled to support voice production.

C

Chest Voice: Quality of the voice where resonance is mostly felt around the chest. It is typically associated with the lower register.

Cilia: hair-like membrane covering the inside of the pharynx and where polluted air is trapped and carried through the breathing and digestive tract.

Classroom Management: a set of skills and strategies defined by the teacher's personality and reflected in the teaching style to organize and structure instruction time and insure that students cooperate and participate positively in order to optimize learning.

D

Decongestant: active ingredient in over-the-counter allergy, common cold and flu virus medications that relaxes and opens up the nose mucous membranes to allow easier breathing and alleviate symptoms of a stuffy nose.

Detoxification: frees the body of harmful substances.

Diaphragm: dome-like muscle at the base of the lungs and attached to the rib cage that control the air pressure coming in and out of the lungs.

Dynamic: the energy required to manipulate and play with a wanted soft or loud voice intonation of the moment.

E

Ego: the perceptive self-conscious. It's that little voice in our head that presses judgment upon our every thought and action.

Enunciation: the art of pronouncing words clearly and effectively.

Exhale: releasing the air out of the lungs.

Exhaustion: extreme fatigue.

F

False Vocal Cords: thick membranes located above the true vocal cords. Whether they are involved in sound production, such as in adding grit to the voice and during extreme screaming is the topic of a hot debate!

Falsetto: typically a light, soft, breathy, undeveloped vocal tone with little resonance in the upper register.

Fixer Elixir: Jaime Vendera's surprisingly quick and efficient home remedy mixture of organic apple cider vinegar, water, organic sea salt, cayenne pepper and organic lemon juice used to prevent or sooth the voice in trouble.

Flu Virus: virus that attacks the respiratory track. Symptoms include nasal congestion, runny nose, sore throat, cough, chest pain, body aches, headache, fever, chills.

Full Voice: a vibrant natural and dynamic vocal tone rich in resonance produced when the voice is properly placed in the mask.

H

Head Voice: higher part of one's register that produces lots of resonance felt in the head.

Histamine: it is released in the body by an allergic reaction and results in dilation of blood vessels, tension in muscles and over-secretion of gastric acid.

Motivation: the will to accomplish something. To be driven to meet a goal.

N

Nodule: little tissue growth on the vocal cords usually caused by repeated vocal fatigue and abuse. They usually appear on the spot of the vocal cords where the most pressure has been applied.

I

Immune System: the body's ability to develop resistance against bacteria, viruses and diseases.

Inhale: action of breathing air in.

Intensity: volume, soft to loud, at which one speaks or sings.

O

Oil of Oregano: plant of the mint family that has antibacterial and anti-inflammatory properties. It can be used to strengthen the immune system.

L

Larynx: pipe in the neck connecting the throat to the lungs and that contains the vocal cords.

Laryngitis: inflammation of the larynx usually caused by a virus or vocal abuse.

P

Pharynx: pipe part of the digestive system that connects the nasal cavity and mouth to the esophagus.

Phlegm: thick mucus secreted in the respiratory tract when there is a presence of irritation caused by voice abuse, a virus or other vocal disorders.

M

Meditation: engage in a mental exercise to still the mind or focus it on a specific reflection in order to bring higher self-awareness or project intent into the future.

Modifying System: composed of the sinus cavities, lips, tongues, pharynx and larynx, they are responsible for vowel and consonant production during speech and singing.

Pitch: the note on which one speaks or sings.

Posture: aligning the body from head to toe!

R

Resonance Chamber: where the voice is most likely to resonate; either in the chest or in the head around the sinus cavities.

Resonating System: the sinus cavities, the tongue, the lips, the pharynx and throat all provide and alter the space needed for the voice to reverberate.

Reverberation: in the vocal context, how the voice echoes in the body.

S

Singing: use the voice to express emotions using melody and musical inflections.

Speaking: express ideas and feelings orally with words.

Sinus Cavities: air-filled spaces in the skull around the nose, behind the cheeks and between, above and behind the eyes that connect the nostrils to the nasal passages and where the voice resonates.

T

Tone Color: the descriptive quality of one's voice: rich, round, thin, vibrant, abrasive, smooth, et cetera.

V

Vibration: in the vocal context, it is the sound energy produced by the trembling or vacillation of the vocal cords.

Vibratory System: the vocal cords and the larynx.

Viral infection: infectious disease caused by a virus that will generally heal on its own over time. Antibiotics are not efficient in treating a disease caused by a virus.

Vocal Cords: two fine mucous membranes located in the larynx that vibrate at a high frequency to produce sounds of different pitches.

Vocal Disorder: a condition that develops over the vocal cords following abusive vocal patterns. Vocal disorders might affect the quality of the sound produced during voicing as well as create discomfort in the throat.

Vocal Range: the wide extent at which someone can sing from the lowest to the highest notes.

Vocal Register: terminology used to describe the comfortable area of notes in which someone speaks or sing (the lower, middle or higher registers). Vocal registers are classified into categories: bass, baritone and tenor for men, and alto, mezzo-soprano and soprano for women.

Voice Placement: area of the body where one chooses to focus the resonance of the voice.

Volume: intensity at which one sings or speaks.

W

Warm-up: a series of short vocal exercises designed to incite brain muscle memory, increase blood flow to the body, develop awareness and prepare the speaker or singer to use his or her voice properly.

Whisper: express ideas with little vibrations of the vocal cords and mostly letting air through the voice box as opposed to producing a clear oral sound.

Y

Yawning: the action of opening the mouth wide and breathing in. Yawning is often the result of slow breathing or fatigue.

Bibliography

Adam, Matt & Vendera, Jaime. "Vocal Mindset", <u>Just for Singers;</u>
<u>This is Your World</u>. December 5th, 2011.
<<u>http://justforsingers.com/products-by-jaime-vendera/</u>>

"Air Supply Mini-Mate Wearable Air Purifier", <u>Wein Products</u>. 1997-
2009 Wein Products Inc. December 5th, 2011.
<<u>http://www.weinproducts.com/minimate.htm</u>>

"Allergy Center: Histamine and Antihistamines", <u>Alpha Online</u>.
Environmed Research Inc. December 5th, 2011.
<<u>http://www.alphanutrition.com/allergy/antihistamines.htm</u>>

"Anatomy and Physiology of Voice Production: Highlights", <u>The Voice</u>
<u>Problem Website</u>. December 5th, 2011.
<<u>http://www.voiceproblem.org/anatomy/index.php</u>>

"Anatomy and Physiology Of Voice Production: Understanding How
Voice Is Produced", <u>The Voice Problem Website</u>. December 5th,
2011.
<<u>http://www.voiceproblem.org/anatomy/understanding.php</u>>

Appell, Thomas. <u>Never Get Another Cold</u>. VDP Publishing, 2004.

Boyle, Amy K. "Noise Center", <u>Center for Hearing and</u>
<u>Communication</u>. 2010 Center for Hearing and Communication.
December 5th, 2011. <<u>http://www.chchearing.org/noise-center-</u>
<u>home/international-noise-awareness-day/sample-press-release</u>>

"Bragg Apple Cider Vinegar", <u>Bragg Health Products and Books</u>.
December 5th, 2011. <<u>http://bragg.com/products/acv.html</u>>

"Brita Products: Faucet Filtration", <u>Brita Water Filtration</u>. December
5th, 2011. <<u>http://www.brita.ca/</u>>

Campbell, Joseph. <u>The Hero with a Thousand Faces</u>. New York, NY.
Princeton University Press, 1949, p. 85–87.

"ChatterVox : The Finest Portable Voice Amplifier", Chatter Vox.
    2009 Asyst Communications Co. December 5th, 2011.
    <http://www.chattervox.com/desc.htm>

"Check Your Meds: Do They Affect Your Voice?", Voice Academy.
    December 5th, 2011. <http://www.uiowa.edu/~shcvoice/rx.html>

"Cold & flu and Vitamin C", C For Yourself. 1997-2008 Cforyourself.
    December 5th, 2011.
    <http://www.cforyourself.com/Conditions/Colds   Flu/colds
    flu.html>

Cooper, Dr Morton. Change Your Voice, Change Your Life. New York,
    NY. Macmillan, 1984.

Cooper, Dr Morton. Change Your Voice, Change Your Life. New York,
    NY. Macmillan, 1984, p. 23

Cross, Melissa. The Zen of Screaming: Vocal Instruction For A New
    Breed. MMV Loudmouth Inc. February 21st, 2007.

Day, Chet. "Chicken Soup: Nature's Best Cold and Flu Remedy?",
    Chet Day's Health & Beyond. 1993-2010 How to Beat Colds and
    Flu with 37 Natural Remedies and Three Healing Meditations.
    December 5th, 2011. <http://chetday.com/coldfluremedy.htm>

"Decibel (dB): Acoustic/Noise", Handbook For Acoustic Ecology.
    1978 World Soundscape Project, Simon Fraser University, and ARC
    Publications. December 5th, 2011. <http://www.sfu.ca/sonic-
    studio/handbook/Decibel.html>

"Diet & Nutrition: Garlic", Health 24. 2000-2010. December 5th,
    2011. <http://www.health24.com/dietnfood/Healthy_foods/15-
    18-20-143.asp>

Dishman, Rod K. "Exercise Fuels The Brain's Stress Buffers",
    American Psychology Association. APA Help Center. December
    5th, 2011. <http://www.apa.org/helpcenter/exercise-stress.aspx>

"Emerita Products: PMS and Peri-Menopause", Emerita. October
    10th, 2010.

<http://www.emerita.com/index.cfm/category/4/perimenopause.cfm>

"Environmental and Workplace Health: Indoor Air Quality – Tools for School Action Kit for Canadian Schools", Health Canada. December 9th, 2007. Government of Canada. December 5th, 2011. <http://www.hc-sc.gc.ca/ewh-semt/pubs/air/tools_school-outils_ecoles/classroom-salle_classe_e.html>

"Food Charts: Alkaline/Acidic Food Charts", The Original Essense-Of-Life LLC. 2002-2010 Raw Food Composition and Nutrition Handbook. December 5th, 2011. <http://www.essense-of-life.com/moreinfo/foodcharts.htm>

Frankl, Viktor E. Man's Search for Meaning. New York, NY. Washington Square Press Publication of Pocket Books, 1959, p.145

Gilbert, Elizabeth. Eat, Pray, Love. New York, NY. Vikin Penguin, 2006, p. 174

Halpern, Sylvie. "Vivre mieux : L'enfant roi", Châtelaine. September 2004 Rogers Media. October 10th, 2010. <http://www.chatelaine.qc.ca/famille/article.jsp?content=200411 08_164016_6516&page=2>

Hunter, Eric J. "153rd ASA Meeting, Salt Lake City, UT. -How Much Do Teachers Talk? Do They Ever Get a Break?" Acoustical Society of America. December 5th, 2011. <http://www.acoustics.org/press/153rd/hunter.html>

Jung, Laurence. "Prévenir l'échec scolaire par une approche globale", Bien Lire! February 2005 CNDP. December 5th, 2011. <http://www.bienlire.education.fr/02-atelier/fiche.asp?theme=1110&id=1362>

Khan, Hazrat Inayat. The Mysticism of Sound and Music. Delhi, India. Motilal Banarsidass Publishers Private Limited, 1990, p. 13

Khan, Hazrat Inayat. The Mysticism of Sound and Music. Delhi, India. Motilal Banarsidass Publishers Private Limited, 1990, p. 77

Khan, Hazrat Inayat. The Mysticism of Sound and Music. Delhi, India. Motilal Banarsidass Publishers Private Limited, 1990, p. 87

Lunau, Kate. "Removing the Accent from Success: An American Helps Immigrants Lose their Accent". Maclean's. July 2nd, 2007. Maclean's Magazine. December 5th, 2011. <http://www.macleans.ca/article.jsp?content=20070702_107049_107049>

"Loud Classroom Hurting Students: Audiologists", CTV. October 1, 2007 CTV Globe Media. December 5th, 2011. <http://www.ctv.ca/servlet/ArticleNews/story/CTVNews/200710 01/noisy_classrooms_071001/20071001?hub=Canada>

Megan "Positively Green". "Get Off the Bottle and On the Filter", Care 2 Make a Difference. September 17th, 2009. Care2. December 5th, 2011. <http://www.care2.com/greenliving/get-off-the-bottle-and-on-the-filter.html>

Mirkin, Dr. Gabe. "How Lack Of Exercises Shortens Lives", Dr Mirkin. January 12, 2001. DrMirkin.com. December 5th, 2011. <http://www.drmirkin.com/fitness/9452.html>

"NasoGel Moisturizer For Dry Noses", NeilMed. 2000-2010 NeilMed Pharmaceutical Inc. December 5th, 2011. <http://www.neilmed.com/can/nasogel.php>

"Nobody At Risk, TB Patient Says", Canada.com. July 12th, 2007. The Windsor Star and CanWest MediaWorks Publications Inc. December 5th, 2011. <http://www.canada.com/nationalpost/news/story.html?id=9203 27a3-838d-4e3c-b641-e2ced7366954>

Oederek, Steve. Evan Almighty. Universal Pictures. USA. June 22nd, 2007.

"Physiological Benefits of Negative Ions on the Human Body", Oriental Detox. December 5th, 2011. <http://www.orientaldetox.com/negative-ions.html>

Ryan, John. "How Laughing is Good for your Health". A World of Good Health. December 5th, 2011.

<http://www.aworldofgoodhealth.com/articles/laughter-for-health.htm>

"Sing", <u>Merriam-Webster Online</u>. December 5th, 2011.
<http://www.merriam-webster.com/dictionary/sing>

"Sinus Rinse TM Nasal Rinse", <u>NeilMed</u>. 2000-2010 <u>NeilMed Pharmaceutical Inc</u>. December 5th, 2011.
<http://www.neilmed.com/can/sinusrinse.php>

"Speak", Merriam-Webster Online. December 5th, 2011.
<http://www.merriam-webster.com/dictionary/speak>

Spears, John. "Going to Town on Bottle Water", <u>The Star</u>. March 8th, 2009. The Toronto Star. December 5th, 2011.
<http://www.thestar.com/news/canada/article/598500#Comments>

"Sunrider: Welcome to Sunrider International", <u>SunRider</u>. 2010 The Sunrider Corporation dba Sunrider International. December 5th, 2011. <www.sunrider.com>

"Teeccino; America's Favorite Coffee Alternative". <u>Teeccino</u>. December 5th, 2011. <http://www.teeccino.com/>

"The Ontario Elementary Curriculum Documents", <u>Ontario Ministry of Education</u>, 2010 Queen's Printer for Ontario. December 5th, 2011. <http://www.edu.gov.on.ca/eng/curriculum/elementary/>

Toombs, Jill. "Cakes By Jill". <u>WordPress</u>. December 5th, 2011.
<http://cakesbyjill.wordpress.com/>

"Understanding the Common Cold: The Nose – Side View", <u>Common Cold</u>. 1999-2007 Commoncold Inc. December 5th, 2011.
<http://www.commoncold.org/undrstnd.htm>

"Useful Information: Histamine Restricted Diet", <u>International Chronic Urticaria Society</u>. December 5th, 2011.
<http://www.chronichives.com/pages/lowhistamine.htm#foodsource>

Vendera, Jaime. "Jaime Vendera : World Class, Glass Shattering Vocal Coach". Jaime Vendera. December 5th, 2011. <www.jaimevendera.com>

Vendera, Jaime. Raise Your Voice; Second Edition. Vendera Publishing, 2007, p.165

Vendera, Jaime. Raise Your Voice; Second Edition. Vendera Publishing, 2007, p.168

Vendera, Jaime. Raise Your Voice; Second Edition. Vendera Publishing, 2007, p. 235

Vendera, Jaime. Raise Your Voice; Second Edition. Vendera Publishing, 2007, p. 264

Werner, Kenny. Effortless Mastery. New Albany, IN. Jamey Aebersold Jazz, Inc., 1996, p. 60

Werner, Kenny. Effortless Mastery. New Albany, IN. Jamey Aebersold Jazz, Inc., 1996, p. 91

Wood Vallely, Sarah. Sensational Meditation for Children. Asheville, NC. Satya Method Resource Center, 2006, p.7

Acknowledgments

I would like to take a moment to show my appreciation to all of those who have contributed to putting this book together... First and foremost: HIM. I feel your love and energy in my heart. You are the source of all life and universal power. I am grateful everyday for every person and experience you put on my path. Because of you, I understand who I am better. I am accepting of the challenges I sometimes face and welcome them as more opportunities to learn. Thank you, God, for teaching me my truth and allowing me to grow and better myself day after day.

To my family: Thank you for being there for me no matter what! My parents Grégoire, Christine and sister Julie: You are my rock of Gibraltar. You give me balance, perspective and strength. *Merci du fond du Coeur!*

Thank you, Jaime Vendera, for believing in me. Your knowledge is impressive, but what I have come to appreciate the most about you is your amazing kindness and generosity. You are an excellent mentor and a wonderful friend. Because of you, I have discovered my full potential as a singer, teacher and writer; you inspire me professionally and personally. You are my brother in music. Thank you for helping me achieve my goals. I couldn't have done it without you!

Thank you, Meagan Ruszyk for all the precious hours you spent editing this book and my online newsletters ever since I have begun this project. I trust you completely with proofreading my work. Pointing out my grammar mistakes and correcting the funny French twists I sometimes put on sentences was very helpful! You have an impeccable eagle eye for the language; you're the best!

To my friends and colleagues: I am so grateful for your ideas and feedback. You showed me that vocal problems were quite common in our teaching community. You initiated in me the will and motivation to share my vocal struggles and solutions. In particular, thank you to the following teachers for your testimonials:

Tristan Cook	Cindy Shore-Beauvais
Liliana Sarno	Rina Banville
Robyn Benjamin	Sheila Peyton Neave
Jill Toombs	

To my young students: I am so proud of all of you who over the years, have set foot in my classroom or crossed my way! Together, we can accomplish so much. As far as we are concerned, the learning experience goes both ways: I will never underestimate the life lessons we share together daily. I love all of your little bursts of joy and academic successes. You help me keep perspective on simple matters of life and remember what happiness is all about. You are my extended family and I love every one of you very dearly.

To my singing teachers, voice students and other musicians I have been lucky enough to work with or meet in interviews: You make me feel in my element! I'm passionate about the voice; and helping each other accomplish ourselves musically, artistically and professionally is rewarding, invigorating and fun! Thank you for the token of trust you put in my vocal and teaching abilities.

I would also like to thank all of you who have taken the time to read this book and spread the word about Voice Yourself in the Classroom! Writing this book for you has been gratifying on multiple levels. It has given me a *raison d'être* and a voice as an author to express myself creatively in a way that I had not attempted before. I discovered more about myself while writing this book than I ever had in my entire life! I am still mystified by the voice—the most intricate and beautiful instrument of all— but I continue to believe in its deep personal connection to and its role in the opening of one's very own soul.

I wish you the best of luck in your vocal endeavors. Speak and sing your heart out! Bless you all!

Biography

Valerie Bastien is a musician at heart and an educator by choice. Formerly trained as a classical singer, she obtained her Baccalaureate in Fine Arts (Specialization Music Performance) from Concordia University in 1998. She also studied classical guitar at Vanier College. If you have ever set foot in Old Montreal during the mid-nineties, you might have heard her coloratura voice resonate throughout *Place Jacques-Cartier* where she was once regularly performing opera arias as a street artist.

Valerie moved to Toronto not long after and put her music projects on hold to reorient her career. She graduated from University of Ottawa in 2003 with a second Baccalaureate in Education. She has since been teaching at the elementary level, and is currently working under the Toronto District School Board. Her focus is on languages (French Immersion) and the arts. Her contributions in these areas include working in collaboration with Chenelière Education in creating the series "Quelle aventure!" on extreme sports targeting young male readers. In 2005, Valerie published a teacher's guide and resource entitled: "Y paraît que...". This complete unit for Grade 7 and 8 French Immersion students is entirely based on the *Television Franco-Ontarienne*'s web-animated Canadian legends of the same title. It provides fun but challenging activities integrating languages (French), technology, visual arts, drama and history.

Faced with the demands of raising her voice constantly to address her class, Valerie soon started struggling with vocal difficulties. This was obviously of great concern to her as singing is her passion. In an effort to terminate her health issues, she dived back into her research of vocal techniques. After realizing that vocal problems were in fact quite common within the teaching community, she was inspired to create the seminar "Voice Yourself in the Classroom!". Her workshop is directly intended to meet the vocal needs of teachers. It offers strategies to find one's natural dynamic speaking voice: a voice that will project easily, feel good, sound great and, of course, last.

Valerie is a vocal coach to the stars and she works with professional musicians in the rock and roll industry. She is a contributor and instructor on RockSource360.com where her interviews with rock stars can be heard and private lessons can be purchased. She is also available for private lessons in person in the Toronto, Ontario area. Contact her on her website for more information. In the series "Voice Yourself", Valerie has recently launched a new website directly addressed to singers: VoiceYourselfForSingers.com, which holds valuable basic information on how to produce a beautiful singing voice.

Writing music is also part of Valerie's creative expression as an artist. She writes pop/folk songs with a world/new age feel that are slightly influenced by her classical training background. Listen to her music at: ValerieBastien.com.

CPSIA information can be obtained at www.ICGtesting.com
Printed in the USA
LVOW071333140213

320066LV00003BA/599/P